Online Resources

Access practical templates of the concepts that you will learn in this book as part of the online resources. These downloadable templates will help you implement your learnings in the real world and give you an in-depth understanding of the concepts.

The templates include:

1. Gantt Chart

2. Time-blocking charts

3. Working backward charts

I0130506

To access the templates, follow the steps below:

1. Go to **www.vibrantpublishers.com**

2. Click on the **'Online Resources'** option on the Home Page

3. Login by entering your account details (or create an account if you don't have one)

4. Go to the Self-Learning Management series section and click on the **'Time Management Essentials You Always Wanted To Know'** link and access the templates.

Happy self-learning!

This page is intentionally left blank

SELF-LEARNING MANAGEMENT SERIES

VIBRANT
PUBLISHERS

TIME MANAGEMENT ESSENTIALS

YOU ALWAYS WANTED TO KNOW

A practical guide to learn managing time at work and in life

DR. ANNAMARIA BLIVEN

Time Management Essentials You Always Wanted To Know
First Edition

Paperback ISBN 10: 1-63651-166-X
Paperback ISBN 13: 978-1-63651-166-5

Ebook ISBN 10: 1-63651-167-8
Ebook ISBN 13: 978-1-63651-167-2

Hardback ISBN 10: 1-63651-168-6
Hardback ISBN 13: 978-1-63651-168-9

Library of Congress Control Number: 2023933110

This publication is designed to provide accurate and authoritative information in regard to the subject matter covered. The Author has made every effort in the preparation of this book to ensure the accuracy of the information. However, information in this book is sold without warranty either expressed or implied. The Author or the Publisher will not be liable for any damages caused or alleged to be caused either directly or indirectly by this book.

Vibrant Publishers books are available at special quantity discount for sales promotions, or for use in corporate training programs. For more information please write to bulkorders@vibrantpublishers.com

Please email feedback / corrections (technical, grammatical or spelling) to spellerrors@vibrantpublishers.com

To access the complete catalogue of Vibrant Publishers, visit www.vibrantpublishers.com

SELF-LEARNING MANAGEMENT SERIES

TITLE	PAPERBACK* ISBN
ACCOUNTING, FINANCE & ECONOMICS	
COST ACCOUNTING AND MANAGEMENT ESSENTIALS	9781636511030
FINANCIAL ACCOUNTING ESSENTIALS	9781636510972
FINANCIAL MANAGEMENT ESSENTIALS	9781636511009
MACROECONOMICS ESSENTIALS	9781636511818
MICROECONOMICS ESSENTIALS	9781636511153
PERSONAL FINANCE ESSENTIALS	9781636511849
ENTREPRENEURSHIP & STRATEGY	
BUSINESS PLAN ESSENTIALS	9781636511214
BUSINESS STRATEGY ESSENTIALS	9781949395778
ENTREPRENEURSHIP ESSENTIALS	9781636511603
GENERAL MANAGEMENT	
BUSINESS LAW ESSENTIALS	9781636511702
DECISION MAKING ESSENTIALS	9781636510026
LEADERSHIP ESSENTIALS	9781636510316
PRINCIPLES OF MANAGEMENT ESSENTIALS	9781636511542
TIME MANAGEMENT ESSENTIALS	9781636511665

*Also available in Hardback & Ebook formats

SELF-LEARNING MANAGEMENT SERIES

TITLE	PAPERBACK* ISBN

HUMAN RESOURCE MANAGEMENT

DIVERSITY IN THE WORKPLACE ESSENTIALS	9781636511122
HR ANALYTICS ESSENTIALS	9781636510347
HUMAN RESOURCE MANAGEMENT ESSENTIALS	9781949395839
ORGANIZATIONAL BEHAVIOR ESSENTIALS	9781636510378
ORGANIZATIONAL DEVELOPMENT ESSENTIALS	9781636511481

MARKETING & SALES MANAGEMENT

DIGITAL MARKETING ESSENTIALS	9781949395747
MARKETING MANAGEMENT ESSENTIALS	9781636511788
SALES MANAGEMENT ESSENTIALS	9781636510743
SERVICES MARKETING ESSENTIALS	9781636511733

OPERATIONS & PROJECT MANAGEMENT

AGILE ESSENTIALS	9781636510057
OPERATIONS & SUPPLY CHAIN MANAGEMENT ESSENTIALS	9781949395242
PROJECT MANAGEMENT ESSENTIALS	9781636510712
STAKEHOLDER ENGAGEMENT ESSENTIALS	9781636511511

*Also available in Hardback & Ebook formats

About the Author

Dr. AnnaMaria Bliven has worked as a business professional for over 30 years gaining experience in business development and management, business improvement, project management, time management, career development and advancement, business strategy, vet-entrepreneurship, team development, teaching and training, and implementation of community projects, and in starting and sustaining for-profit and not-for-profit businesses.

As a seasoned business owner and a master at managing time, her goals are to share lessons and best practices for starting, sustaining, and succeeding in business ventures, and leveling up in career fields. To that end, she meets with clients on a regular basis assisting them with achieving their career and business goals. Dr. Bliven started her career as a Certified Travel Consultant while in the Army National Guard and served a total of 26 years with combined service in the Army National Guard, Army, and Army Reserve in the career fields of music, human resources, education services, and career development. She achieved her certification as a Global Career Development Facilitator in addition to becoming a Data Analyst and a college instructor. She has an undergraduate degree in Communication from Arizona State University, a Master of Arts degree in Communication from West Virginia University, a Master's in Business Administration from Colorado Technical University-online, and a Doctorate in Business Administration from the University of Wisconsin-Whitewater. She is also the author of Business Plan Essentials You Always Wanted To Know.

Other Contributors

Julie A. DeSot, DM, has a Doctorate in Management from the University of Maryland Global Campus. She has over ten years of instructional experience and 26 years of professional experience in leadership, management, and project/program management. Dr. DeSot helps individuals and organizations improve their performance through process improvement, professional development, and consulting. She also has professional memberships in Project Management Institute (PMI) and MyAxelos.

What experts say about this book!

Dr. AnnaMaria Bliven commits to honoring your time, being intentional about it, and enhancing your effectiveness in managing it... and she succeeds! She highlights insights from a variety of sources and expands on her own insightful ideas to effectively manage this invaluable resource. As a consummate educator, she includes tools and resources that will add to your successful integration of her ideas into your busy lives. Additional resources, effective in reinforcing the concepts and ideas while helping you to act include learning objectives, templates, charts, and suggested printouts to post/use, along with learning objectives, chapter summaries, concrete examples, author's anecdotes, acronyms, and quizzes. These resources will help you to best understand and implement her ideas and integrate them into your time management practices. And you do want to implement them. As an accomplished academic, her references and citations give you additional access to other appropriate sources as well. Though many of her insights might be considered common sense, especially after you read them, you end up realizing that they are not so common. Whether you are an employee, student, parent, or manager wishing you had more time, your dreams can come true. Take control of your time and make up for the lost time. It's time to not only read this book but take action to enhance your path to success by applying these ideas and insights today! Read and implement ideas found in this practical guide.

Wishing you intentionality and positivity, as encouraged in this book. Thank you, Dr. Bliven for sharing and inspiring!

– Scott Dell, Assistant Professor,
School of Business, Francis Marion University

Nicely formatted book and an easy approach to time management.

– Sabra Brock, Chair, Department of Business & Accounting,
Touro University New York School of Career and Applied Studies

What experts say about this book!

This book reflects on the aspects every one of us never tried but wanted to. It ensures that we all can control time when we plan. Each section teaches some methods that helps to manage time under various scenarios. The simple explanations with examples are helpful to understand how to manage time easily for all types of audience. This is certainly an asset for students to avoid wasting time in unwanted activities and take control over it.

– Dr.Mohanasundari Thangavel, Assistant Professor (Economics), Indian Institute of Technology Indore

This book will be beneficial to students, professionals, mid-level managers, startup founders to manage their time.

– Prof Ruchi Arya, Assistant Professor, Shri Vaishnav Vidyapeeth Vishwavidyalaya, Indore

Working Backwards and Time-Blocking charts are useful tips given by the author. The quizzes at the end of every chapter are a nice way to recall the chapter.

– Dr. Vidhya Darshan Thakkar, Assistant Professor, K J Somaiya Institute of Management

Table of Contents

Part 2 Time Management for the Remote Worker   63

This page is intentionally left blank

Preface

A precious commodity we have in our lives is TIME. This is the dash between the date we arrive in this world to the date we leave it. How we spend this commodity, how we save this commodity, and how we maximize this commodity is what this book is all about. Living a life with little or no regrets is the ultimate goal of most people's lives. Making use of time in the manner desired is how a person can be satisfied at the end of life, knowing that the time spent was what they wanted to spend it on and accomplish the things they wanted to achieve.

Many people scramble for time in their daily life. While writing this book, it was a déjà vu moment remembering moments from my life when it became clear that time spent correctly netted many positive outcomes. So, I conducted intentional observation as to how my time was being spent and documented this information for over two years, and carefully analyzed it. From this analysis, it was apparent how to ensure that I spent my time wisely. In addition, I also learned how to schedule and organize activities and events for both personal and professional reasons from several companies in which I worked.

It did not take very long before the results of taking specific actions to preserve time and prevent the loss of time started to occur. My days were fulfilling and satisfying. The fulfilled days accompanied fulfilled feelings. Knowing the techniques used to preserve and protect time will help you schedule and organize moments in the day that will result in multiple positive outcomes.

This page is intentionally left blank

Introduction to the book

This book is the ultimate guide to never asking "where did the time go?" and having less stressful and more blissful days. Most of the time slips away or gets wasted due to not managing, monitoring, and controlling the moments in the day. We realize time has slipped by us with the unintentional consequences of not monitoring the moments in the day. What do we mean by "unintentional consequences?" We are referring to things that need improvement due to poor planning or poor follow-up and follow-through. If time is allowed to slip by without the intentional use of it, you may miss out on visiting friends and family or taking a vacation, miss a deadline for the application to get into the college you wanted, miss the deadline for the application to apply for the job you wanted, ... you get the drift. If we are not watchful and mindful of our time, it tends to fly by unchecked. By intentionally making each moment accounted for, you can always know how your time is spent and where you spent it. Michael Altshuler said it best: "The bad news is time flies. The good news is you're the pilot."[1]

Time management is managing activities from when a person is awake and alert to when they close their eyes and drift asleep. Mastering the moments in the day and making the most of them may sound complicated, but it's not. It takes the mindset to live to make every moment of every day count and accomplish a task, goal, or objective. Whatever you want for your life is attainable when you spend your time wisely.

Each chapter in this book gives tips, tricks, and techniques for how to use and manage time to a person's advantage. The

---

1. Finn, Amy (2022) 140 Time Quotes on Making Every Second Count. *Quote Ambition.* Retrieved from www.quoteambition.com

tips, tricks, and techniques are thoroughly explained and include practical scenarios.

By the end of this book, you will be able to answer the following questions regarding the techniques to use for using time wisely and not wasting it.

- What is time management?
- How to not waste time?
- What to do when time is lost?
- How to stretch time in a day?

Average time spent by adults 18+ years of age on media:

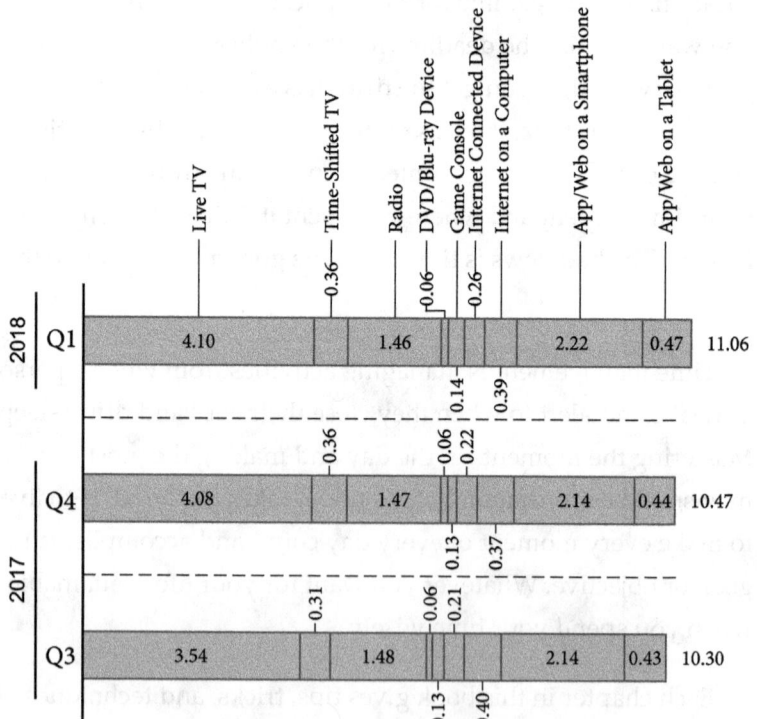

	Live TV	Time-Shifted TV	Radio	DVD/Blu-ray Device	Game Console	Internet Connected Device	Internet on a Computer	App/Web on a Smartphone	App/Web on a Tablet	Total
2018 Q1	4.10	1.46	0.36	0.06		0.26		2.22	0.47	11.06
					0.14		0.39			
2017 Q4	4.08	1.47	0.36	0.06	0.22			2.14	0.44	10.47
					0.13		0.37			
2017 Q3	3.54	1.48	0.31	0.06	0.21			2.14	0.43	10.30
					0.13		0.40			

Source: www.nielsen.com

Time is relative

Figure above shows us how we, on average, spend our day. What we value most is what we tend to spend the most time on. Albert Einstein stated, "Time is relative; its only worth depends upon what we do as it is passing."[2] Einstein was referring to the moments we experience as we are awake and what we do with them. It is based on a person's frame of reference. This relativity also refers to a measure between moments.

Master the moments in the day

Mastering the moments in the day takes skill and practice. Mohammed Khan said, "If you can master your mind, you can master your time."[3] It takes a mindset with the intention to see and preplan for the activities in advance of the event taking place. In this book, there are many examples of using the mindset of intentionality, preplanning, and pro-action prior to an event so as to not waste time or create moments of dread and disaster.

Making the most of time

Charles Buxton stated, "You will never find time for anything. If you want time, you must make it."[4] Another pertinent statement made by Bud Bilanich makes us pause and ponder: "Time is a scarce and non-renewable resource."[5] This implies that this scarce and non-renewable resource should be used prudently and not be wasted.

---

2. Quote from Albert Einstein

3. Khan, Mohammed (2016) *Mastering Your Time*. CreateSpace Independent Publishing Platform, 62 pages ISBN-10: 1533070113; ISBN-13: 978-1533070111.

4. Khan, Mohammed (2016) *Mastering Your Time*. CreateSpace Independent Publishing Platform, 62 pages ISBN-10: 1533070113; ISBN-13: 978-1533070111.

5. Bilanich, Bud (2008) Spend Your Time on The Things That Are Important for Your Success. *Fast Company*. Retrieved from www.fastcompany.com

In *Psychology Today,* Dr. Marty Nemko, PhD., gives six secrets to making the most of time: (1) Realize you'll feel better if you get more done, (2) Be time-conscious, (3) Be time-effective, (4) Consciously decide if you want to pursue a significant time snatcher (i.e., playing video games, perusing the social media postings timeline, etc.), (5) Delegate, (6) Always have a "sponge activity" (when in a waiting stance) at the ready.[6] In essence, take intentional mental and physical actions to spend time wisely and productively.

Managing moments in the day like a game

There are two rules to this game, and they are (1) not to waste time and (2) not to create moments of stress, dread, or regret. No one enjoys moments when time is wasted. To win this game, the player must take their turn. Their turn begins with thinking of ways to take action that are positive and productive. These actions prevent a person from wasting time and having moments of stress, dread, or regret.

The player begins their turn thinking of what they wish to accomplish in the allotted time from when they wake up to when they go to sleep. For some, the day begins in the morning; for some, it starts at noon. In any case, how the time is spent is for the player to decide. Each moment of the day, when the time is spent acting, counts as a move forward in life. Acting, such as creating a plan toward accomplishing a goal, objective, or mission in life or at work, will no doubt result in a positive and productive outcome for the player and all those people in the player's workplace and family life. Winning the game takes intention, determination, and lots of practice.

---

6. Nemko, Marty (2014) Six Secrets to Making the Most of Your Time. *Psychology Today.* Retrieved from www.psychologytoday.com

Who can benefit from this book?

- Students who want to stay on track with their coursework and stay caught up.

- Parents that are juggling work and family obligations with various schedules.

- Professionals juggling various schedules, including home, work, business, and community obligations and want to stay on track for meeting personal and professional goals.

- Anyone who wants always to be prepared to have events in life take place without a hitch.

This page is intentionally left blank

How to use this book?

This book can be used as a guide to understanding and applying the techniques for saving and making the most of time. This book is a must-read for students, professionals, and entrepreneurs who want to learn how to manage their time between various obligations.
For making the most out of this book:

- Read the various time management methods given in the book and try to implement them in your daily life.

- Take a printout of the Gantt chart, fill it, and stick it on their wall.

- Get a template of the time-blocking chart and recreate it using a spreadsheet to plan out the time in the day to get tasks for home, work, and whatever else done.

- Use the charting for task listing and task completion to think through what is needed to be fully prepared for an event taking place.

This page is intentionally left blank

Part 1: Time Management for ALL

P art 1 covers key topics about mastering, managing, and monitoring our time. The purpose is to ensure time never gets away from us, or if it does, what to do to find where it went and bring it back.

The key learning objectives include:

- Understanding and appreciating time as a gift to be used and not wasted

- How to master time in the day so it is never lost

- How to work backward to ensure time is used wisely

- Using momentary monitoring to ensure where the time is going

- How to manage expectations

- How to find the time that may be lost

Time is a gift. It is not something one has to work for and earn. Cheryl Rich said, "time is a gift that most of us take for granted." We get so caught up in our daily lives that we rarely stop and take a serious look at how we are spending this gift."[7] Every moment we are awake and alert, we have time. It is for use in any way seen fit. However, if not managed properly, the gift of time is wasted.

Wasted time is of no benefit to anyone. It is frustrating when you realize that you have wasted your time. So, in the interest of limiting those moments of frustration, knowing some tips, tricks, and techniques for using time and not wasting it would be very beneficial, wouldn't it?

Chapter **1**

Tips for Mastering Time in the Day

> Key learning objectives should include the reader's understanding of the following:
>
> - How working backward is a smart time investment
>
> - How you will always be prepared for scheduled events
>
> - How to not waste time redoing something or going back for an item left at home or your office by error
>
> - How working backward in time saves us from wasting time or having embarrassing moments

The military teaches leaders to use "work backward in time"[8] to ensure that all aspects of a mission are well thought out and planned. All facets of the mission, including contingencies, are anticipated and can be handled should the need arise. It's like creating a Gantt chart listing all the actions that must occur ahead of the scheduled date. Henry Laurence Gantt, a highly respectable

---

8. Author's personal experience.

project management scholar in the 1920s, created the Gantt Chart to keep track of projects within a span of time. A Gantt chart begins with the day of the event or activity to the right of the paper, filling in the rest of the chart, and working from the right to the left of the scheduled date, creating prior dates with a specific action that takes place in preparation for the activity or event.

A Gantt chart gets created the moment you schedule an event on the calendar. This chart is not just used by a business or school professionals and project managers. In fact, this chart is used for planning anything that requires preparation. Going to the theatre or shopping would not necessarily require the use of a Gantt Chart. But, taking a trip to Europe, camping with the family, or moving to a new location for work or school takes preparation for the tasks in advance. It will feel awkward at first. However, after using this method constantly and consistently experiencing the ecstatic feeling of being fully prepared, you will want to use this technique to always be prepared. The more prepared you are, the less stressed you feel and the more enjoyment you experience.

Creating a Gantt Chart is a simple form of preparing and planning all the items and taskings it takes for the event to occur without a hitch.

Table 1.1   Example of a Gantt Chart

Tasks for camping on July 22-25				
(Planning and preparing starts from April 15)	April 15-30	May 1-31	June 1-30	July 1-22
Make a reservation for a camping spot	▓			
Purchase camping equipment: sleeping bags, pads, blankets, pillows, toiletries	▓			
Check inventory of fishing equipment	▓			
Purchase needed fishing gear		▓		
Purchase ice-chests		▓		
Make a list and purchase food items				▓

This technique goes something like this for long-range time management:

The family plans to go camping in the woods with other family members and friends. The date for this event is in four months. Planning and preparing backward starts with the day of the event and working backward in time. We begin by visualizing that the car is packed with sleeping bags, pads, blankets, pillows, food, snacks, drinks, and clothing. Since other members of this party are bringing the tents, ingredients for smores, and for starting a fire, that is covered. However, in this scenario, this family likes to go fishing and will need the tackle box, fishing poles, net, a bag for the fish caught, and fishing bait. Now, all these items must be available and packed on the day of the event. Here is what happens before that…

One or two days before the camping trip, the family goes shopping for food, drinks, and paper items and gets the fishing bait. Next, they arrange sleeping bags with pads, blankets, and pillows to be sure each person is comfortable while sleeping in the tents. They also make sure the ice chests have sufficient ice and space for all the perishable food items.

An inventory takes place one to two months before the day of the event, making sure that all the items for camping in tents are accounted for. As the inventory check takes place, it is discovered that one of the sleeping bags is attacked by an animal and needs to be replaced. One fishing pole reel is broken, and the tackle box is missing some bobbers. Now the family makes a trip to the store to buy a new sleeping bag, a reel for the fishing pole, and a pack of bobbers.

One month before the event's day, the family plans the camping trip's menu and they list down all food and paper items. The ice chests are brought down from the shelves in the garage and inspected for cleanliness.

In this scenario, all items needed for camping and fishing are on hand, not broken, ripped, or missing. By working backward in time, there are no nasty surprises on the day of the event that could waste time and turn the event into a disastrous and very stressful one.

Planning and preparing for a family camping trip to go smoothly is a reason for using this technique. However, this technique can be applied to more straightforward occasions too. Here is another example of working backward in time purposefully to wisely spend a Saturday…

You have four hours to spend on a Saturday while the kids are at a sports event. You have to clean the closets, do gardening, and repair a screen door before it is time to pick up the kids. Working backward, it takes twenty minutes to drive to where the kids need to be picked up at noon that day. Here is how to plan and account for the three hours and forty minutes.

Of the three tasks, gardening takes the least amount of time taking approximately fifteen minutes. Do that first. Next, repairing the screen will take around twenty minutes since all the materials to fix the screen are in one place in the garage. After fixing the screen, cleaning the closets is the next task. In this scenario, there are approximately two hours and twenty minutes to clean out the closet. If it takes less time, it gives you more time to relax, do a floor sweep or watch TV, play a game, or just drive over to where the kids are and watch them having fun.

According to an article written by Atanu Chaudhuri in SureSolv, working backward to solve a problem is also prudent. In cases where there is a target destination with a target time, this technique comes in handy.[9] A person with an appointment to meet someone, take an exam, appear in court, or get married needs to have the transportation figured out and whatever else is needed for the event to go as planned.

---

9. Retrieved from www.suresolv.com

Working backward does not happen easily. It takes determination and discipline to want to do it. Can you see the value of working backward from the examples in this chapter?

Working backward also takes practice. The more you do it, the better you get at it. With practice and time, you begin to naturally start the thought process with what needs to take place and when it needs to take place as it relates to the event about to take place. Such as the time allotted in the day before picking someone up, the time before going to work, or attending a meeting. Take notice of the amount of time blocked in which you can do what needs to be done.

Another case when this technique is beneficial is when you are taking online college courses, and also have a new job with greater job responsibilities. As a college student, you have scheduled assignments, and as an employee, there are expected deliverables. It may seem difficult to juggle all these responsibilities without anything falling to the ground. But by using the technique of working backward, it is possible to fulfill your school, work, and family obligations.

The college student with work and family obligations can juggle all the responsibilities with confidence, knowing that all the tasks associated with school, work, and home are taken care of.

Working backward happens with intention. It takes internal motivation to follow through with the plan and to prepare for an event, take a trip, move to a new location, start college, or any other activity. You can use the working backward technique to avoid nasty surprises that can waste time and spoil the activity. It makes for a bad experience; for example, reaching the airport but realizing that you don't have your passport. Or, moving into your dorm at college and realizing that you forgot something at home that would have added to your comfort in the dorm or apartment.

The best way to prevent moments of dread that come after learning you are missing something is to make sure you have everything you need and want for the trip, activity, or event. By working backward, you have time to think about what is needed, take the steps to ensure what is needed is attended to, and have all the elements it takes for the event or activity.

Still not convinced and wondering if working backward is worth it? Read this anecdote.

Author's Anecdote

I have experienced many times that when planning backward would have been the correct course of action, it was overlooked. One time, I had to drive back to my house three times in one weekend because critical supplies were missing on a nice camping trip (i.e., cookware, bedding, recreational items, medication for the dog, etc.). Thankfully, the distance between my house and the campground was only 22 miles (one-way) but think of the wasted time that I would otherwise have used for boating on the lake, taking a hike through the woods, playing a card game, or just sitting, relaxing, and enjoying being in the fresh air outdoors.

Before learning how to work backward to ensure all needed tasks and items are done in time for the scheduled event, I experienced many occasions where I had to make three trips back to the house, resend an email, apologize for omitting crucial information or statements, charts, graphs, etc. This wasted a lot of my time and energy. Wasting and losing time causes stress, disappointment, and regret. Finally, I got to the point where I resolved to ensure that no more time is wasted or lost. I learned how to work backward. It is a natural thing to do when faced with an upcoming scheduled event, whether it is an event for business, work, or for personal reasons.

Working backward and thinking about the tasks that need to be done is like being your clock dial. As you are doing what you planned and intended to do within the allotted time, you know for sure you are in control, seeing where the time went and how it is being spent. Not only that, but most people also feel satisfied that their time is spent wisely, which gives them a feeling of fulfillment.

So, you might wonder, how exactly do I get started learning and practicing "working backward?" Here is a simple exercise to get you started.

Exercise 1

Begin by looking at your calendar and seeing the next scheduled event.

What is that date? Write down the date in this matrix.

Table 1.2   **Table of working backward for planning a trip to Italy**

Event	(What is the event?)	Traveling to Italy for two weeks
Date of the event	(When is the event taking place)	June 21
Reason or purpose of the event	(What is the reason or purpose of the event?)	Visiting family and traveling
Things needed for the event	(What things do you need for the event?)	Gifts for family members, appropriate clothing and walking shoes, camera with a selfie stick, extra suitcase, etc.

Now that we know when the event is taking place, where it is taking place, and what its reason or purpose is, we can turn our attention to what we need to have with us on this trip and make a timeline to go along with the list. For this example, we know that you purchased the plane ticket three months before taking this trip, and it is April 1st. In this scenario, you have from April 1 to June 21 to be fully prepared for the trip to Italy.

Table 1.3	Table for working backward with tasks and deadlines for trip to Italy

Tasks that need to be done	Resources to get the task done	Deadline to complete
Make sure passport is up to date	US Customs Office	April 5
Purchase plane ticket	Online airline site	April 10
Research destinations to tour in Italy	Internet, ask family members in Italy	May 1
Purchase rail pass	Online rail pass - internet	June 1
Buy a decent pair of comfortable walking shoes	Research online and onsite shoe sales options	June 1
Learn Italian (basic level)	Rosetta Stone	June 11
Purchase gifts for family	Maple Leaf Cheese and Wine Shop	June 15
Create a packing list		June 19
Pack the suitcase		June 20

Here is what a Gantt Chart for preparing to take the trip to Italy looks like:

Table 1.4   Gantt Chart for Taking a Trip to Italy

Tasks for traveling to Italy on June 21				
(Starting March 10)	March 10 – 30	April 1 – 30	May 1 – 31	June 1 – 21
Get passport	▓			
Research destinations in Italy	▓			
Purchase plane tickets		▓		
Purchase Euro rail pass		▓		
Buy comfortable walking shoes		▓	▓	
Learn Italian (basic level)	▓	▓		
Purchase gifts for family members		▓	▓	
Create packing list			▓	
Pack the suitcase				▓

Of course, we take these measures so that the trip to Italy goes well with no hiccups or stressful moments. Can you imagine feeling embarrassed showing up without a gift for your family because you forgot it or not having your rail pass? Or regretting not buying comfortable walking shoes after your feet hurt from walking all day?

This is just an exercise to help you with the practical application of working backward. After doing this a few times, you might not even need this matrix. You will know what needs to be done, calendar it, and get it done accordingly.

After you do this and experience the thrill of an activity, or event with no nasty surprises, you will be addicted to this habit of planning and preparing. You will always want to plan for scheduled activities or events by planning backward.

Discussion Questions

1. Can you recall an event for which you were unprepared?

2. Did you ever wish there was a way to always remember having the needed items for an event to run smoothly for you and your family?

3. After reading this chapter, what do you plan to do to ensure you are always prepared?

Quiz

━━━━━━━━━━━━━━━━━━━━━━━━━━━━━━━━━━━━━

1. **Two outcomes when implementing the technique of working backward in time are:**

   a. Intentionality and productivity

   b. Momentarily monitoring and productivity

   c. Not wasting time and not asking, "where did the time go"

2. **_____ takes time to learn and implement.**

   a. Productive planning

   b. Working backward

   c. Intentional determination

3. **Time is a _____.**

   a. virtue

   b. value

   c. gift

4. **Not _____ time is the ultimate goal for having a life of no regrets.**

   a. wasting

   b. having

   c. needing

5. **There is never enough time to do the things you want to do.**

   a. True

   b. False

6. **Working backward does not happen _____.**

   a. easily

   b. on its own

   c. overnight

7. **Working backward begins with _____.**

   a. where the event takes place

   b. why the event is occurring

   c. on which date the event is scheduled to take place.

8. **When and where the event is to take place matters when working backward.**

   a. True

   b. False

9. **Working backward and thinking about the tasks need to be done is like _____.**

   a. being your own clock dial

   b. being in control of your destiny

   c. being smart

10. According to an article written by Atanu Chaudhuri in
    SureSolv, working backward to solve a problem is also
    _____.

    a. prudent

    b. perfect

    c. promising

Answers	1 – c	2 – b	3 – c	4 – a	5 – b
	6 – a	7 – c	8 – a	9 – a	10 – a

Chapter Summary

◆ There are ways to ensure that your life with all its scheduled events goes smoothly.

◆ Working backward is how people strategize, plan, and prepare for events ahead of when they are scheduled to take place. By doing this, they are likely to have less stress and enjoy life better than waiting until the last minute and not being prepared.

◆ Working backward is doing tasks associated with preparing for the event months, days, or hours before the event is set to occur.

◆ Working backward allows understanding the event's when, what, why, and where and plan for what is needed at the event.

This page is intentionally left blank

Chapter **2**

Techniques and Tricks to Use for Monitoring Moments in Your Day

Key learning objectives should include the reader's understanding of the following:

- How to have fulfilling and highly productive days every day

- How to always be prepared with materials, resources, etc., for any planned and scheduled event

- How to manage and monitor where your time is spent every day

- How to remain in control of the time each day

- How to preserve and protect your work and family relationships

Being one's clock dial while working backward in time is a neat technique. Intentionally doing it is a trick that makes it possible to monitor where time goes. It is one thing to "think of what needs to be done," it is quite another thing to "do what needs to be done." Therefore for this method to be fully effective, it takes both intentionality and productivity. It takes thought and then action. So, let's deal with the thinking part first.

How many times in a week, month, or year does the thought, "I wish I had more time, occur?" Using the trick of intentionality and productivity, it is possible to stretch the time each day, starting with a thought. Thinking that each day is filled with productivity that counts is the first step to having fulfilling days. That may seem way too simplistic but it is challenging for most people. Especially for people who are just "marking time" waiting for something to happen to them. Marking time is when a person is intentionally not engaged in a task of some kind, either as an employment task, a home chore, a school or business, or an action taken toward a future plan. Nonengagement in life is "marking time." When soldiers mark time in a march, they are not moving forward, just moving their feet and legs up and down in the same spot. Once again, not moving forward is the same as wasting time if there is no intended purpose for marking time.

One trick for controlling time while marking it and monitoring it is intentionality. Keeping your leisurely pursuits within a time limit is one way of managing time and monitoring moments in the day. An example is, "After taking a two-week break after leaving this job, I will look for another job." During the two-week break, each day is filled with activities like watching movies on Netflix or video gaming. In this situation, this is not considered as time wasted but rather time spent relaxing and regrouping. It could even be considered a form of productivity as you become more relaxed after doing the activities.

Productivity is another trick for staying in control of time and momentarily monitoring while not marking time. Now let's revisit the nagging question on most people's minds throughout the year – "I wish I had more time [to do what?]." Hearing this makes one wonder, what would a person do with more time? When a person is coming closer to the end of their time on earth and passing away, they rarely say, "I wish I had more money or more things." No, they say, "I wish I had more time."

Thinking in advance of what tasks, goals, objectives, or even missions a person wishes to accomplish is the first thing that takes place. Next are the actions that follow the thought. Using the trick of productivity to control and monitor one's time ensures that there is no wasted time and no regrets at the end of one's lifetime. Here is an example of how the technique of intentionality and productivity and working backward in time are used...

Joe wants to attend a school for learning motorcycle mechanics. He wants to own a motorcycle shop and garage eventually. He graduates with an associate degree in English. He works at a pizzeria making pizzas to pay the bills and is a backup delivery driver. Now, using intentionality and productivity tricks, with the combination of working backward in time, Joe spends the summer preparing to attend the technical vocational school in the fall. Since he works in the afternoon and early evening hours with two days off per week, Joe wisely makes use of his mornings and later evenings to identify which school will he attend, apply for scholarships and grants, and get the study material in advance (available online) to take and pass the tests to be ASE Certified after taking the classes. Joe is determined to do well in his classes and pass the ASE Certification test on his first attempt. Using the intentionality trick makes it possible to think about when to go online, find the right school, and do what is required for admission. Using the productivity trick makes it possible for him to know how many hours it takes to read and review the materials to take and pass the ASE Certification exam on the first attempt. Using the technique of working backward makes it possible for Joe to plan in advance what he will need in the dorm room and how much funds are required to cover costs associated with tuition, books, class fees, food, clothing, supplies, gas for the car to drive to the campus location, etc. In this scenario, from the thought of attending school to the actual arrival on campus, each moment was monitored and managed, allowing for a less stressful experience while at school.

Let's use this same technique for planning a weekend.

Case example: Mary and Tom both work full-time jobs outside the home Monday through Friday. They have always wanted to maximize the hours on the weekend but always come up short by Sunday night. Almost every Sunday night, they are sad and depressed and ask each other, "where did the time go?" They feel that with all the time that they had on the weekend, they got nothing worthwhile accomplished. For most people, a weekend starts Friday night and ends on Sunday night; the same is true for Mary and Tom.

Applying the technique of working backward with intentionality and productivity, here is how the weekend can go for Mary and Tom, having them feel fulfilled on Sunday night.

This example continues with the first step: knowing what Mary and Tom want to accomplish during their weekend. Mary always wanted to plant a flower garden in front of their house, and Tom always wanted to build a patio with a fire pit in the backyard.

The next step is to answer the questions using the template from Chapter 1.

Table 2.1	**Table for working backward for planting a flower garden**

Event	(What is the event?)	Planting a flower garden
Date of the event	(When is the event taking place)	May 10
Reason or purpose of the event	(What is the reason or purpose of the event?)	For the beauty of it
Things needed for the event	(What things do you need for the event?)	Flower plants Something to feed the plants Mulch Garden utilities

Tasks that need to be done	Resources to get the task done	Deadline to complete
Research the types of flower plants that work for the area where the home is located (For example, cactus plants would not do well in Northern Michigan)	Internet	April 10
Measure the area where the garden will be planted and make sure to get enough plants and mulch	Measuring tape or stick	April 15
Purchase flower plants	Store with gardening section	April 20
Purchase garden gloves	Store with gardening section	April 20
Purchase garden utilities (spade, rake, shovel)	Store	April 20
Research the item to feed the plants	Internet	April 19
Purchase the item to feed the plants	Store with gardening section	April 20

Answering the when, what, where, and why questions and then making a list of the tasks to do in preparation for planting the garden makes it possible to have every item in place when planting a garden. If Tom is not helping Mary plant the garden, then at the same time, he can work on making the patio with the fire pit in the backyard. Tom can ensure that all the items needed are handy before that day in the same manner Mary did.

Ironically, sitting down with this matrix of questions takes some time to work backward with intentionality. However, can you sense the return on investment of this time and effort? There is less stress and more productivity. In addition, the activity or event goes smoothly when you are fully ready and prepared.

It is an investment of time to not waste time. That may sound strange, but when this technique is fully implemented, and you experience the joy of attending a scheduled activity or event with pre-planning, you will want to continue this form of planning and preparing for any event or activity. This will become an instinct whenever there is something you are planning to attend and do.

By implementing this technique, you are ensuring that the activity or event takes place without a glitch. Imagine using this time-saving technique every time you have a scheduled activity or event taking place. You arrive at the event or start the event with all it takes to have a great time with nothing missing. The opposite is experiencing a tough time dealing with moments of dread of missing something.

Monitoring the day to be sure that what you intend to do is done gives you confidence knowing that all the bases are covered. To honor all commitments and responsibilities is an issue when you have multiple responsibilities, such as college, work, and home. If you have one or more children on a sports team, there are practice times and games scheduled that take time and preparation too. Planning to have the uniforms cleaned, sports equipment in good repair and properly fitted, and the children well prepared with their heads in the game all takes time, effort, and energy. Intentionally using the working backward technique, you and the kids can get to the sports event completely ready to do your part for the team. Imagine arriving at the soccer field straight from the classroom with a duffle bag missing the shin guards. If that were to happen, your child would be missing an essential part of their uniform and equipment and thus sitting on the bench rest of the game. Instead, the duffle bag has all the equipment needed and the child is ready to play the game.

Take a moment and read the Author's Anecdote and see what happens when the technique of working backward with intentionality is *not* used.

Author's Anecdote

There was a weekend when I wanted to plant a garden on a Saturday but did not use the working backward technique. Here is what happened…

Instead of having a whole day to plant the garden, the morning was spent at the store purchasing flower, vegetable plants, and plant food. It was an hour's drive between the store and the house. Without the proper planning that comes with working backward, I didn't have a list of things needed before going to the store. So, you guessed it. When I returned home, I only bought the plants and plant food and forgot the garden utensils or garden gloves. Seeing that, I went back to the store. Now, three hours of the Saturday had elapsed.

After returning from the store with the garden utensils and garden gloves, thinking that all the needed items were now at hand, I paused the project to have lunch, confident that after lunch, the garden would be planted as planned.

While having lunch, I had an afterthought to "YouTube" and see how a garden is planted. That's when the mulching part of growing a garden came into play. By this time, the Saturday was well into the afternoon. I was now furious at myself and sorely disappointed that the garden project was not going as planned. The next day, Sunday, it poured the entire day. By Sunday night, feelings of sadness took over the night. This could have all been avoided by working backward.

Discussion Questions

1. What is an upcoming project or event that you are preparing for?

2. What are the necessary items you need to accomplish your project or run your event?

3. What do you need to do (tasks) and have (materials) to accomplish your project/event?

4. Using the planning matrix and working backward, how are you feeling knowing that you are covering all the bases for the project or event?

Quiz

1. **Thinking that each day is filled with productivity that counts is the first step to having fulfilling days.**

   a. True

   b. False

2. **A tip for making sure things are getting done to have a smooth event or a completed project without hiccups is to:**

   a. Work backward

   b. Hope for the best

   c. Leave it to fate

3. **People feel more _____ and satisfied with their lives when all their obligations are met.**

   a. fulfilled

   b. productive

   c. sad

4. **While marking time, it is possible to also be _____.**

   a. productive

   b. complacent

   c. none of the above

5. **By working backward with intentionality and productivity, a person can experience _____.**

   a. being fully prepared for an event or completing a project

   b. feeling fulfilled and not frustrated

   c. both of these answers are correct

6. **Intentionality means _____.**

   a. having a strong desire and intention to get something done

   b. maybe there will be time to get something done

   c. none of these answers are correct

7. **Productivity is something that _____.**

   a. happens with intentionality

   b. someone can only wish that will happen

   c. it Is not something that happens all the time

8. **Working backward with intentionality leads to productivity.**

   a. True

   b. False

9. **It takes _____ to sit down with a matrix of questions in preparing for an event or a project.**

   a. willingness

   b. time

   c. way power

10. Working backward can happen without intentionality.

    a. True

    b. False

Answers	1 – a	2 – a	3 – b	4 – a	5 – c
	6 – a	7 – a	8 – a	9 – b	10 – b

Chapter Summary

◆ Working backward with intentionality is followed by productivity.

◆ Having the intention to work backward helps provide the discipline to use this technique to save time and not waste time.

◆ It takes intentionality to follow through with the set schedule of tasks to accomplish goals.

This page is intentionally left blank

Chapter **3**

Tricks to Use for Being in Control of Time: Managing Expectations

Key learning objectives should include the reader's understanding of the following:

- How to never waste time pondering over things that cannot be changed

- How to manage expectations for yourself and others

- How to not lose time with negative thoughts

- How to remain in control of reactions to happenstances

- How to preserve and protect your emotions and energies

Another source of frustration and waste of time is the **expectation** associated with time. Expecting a specific thing to happen in a certain amount of time, and when it does not happen, is frustrating. Just take a moment and reflect on the times when you were so angry and disappointed you could not think straight.

At that moment, you were so consumed with these thoughts and emotions that you were not able to move forward in doing or saying anything. At that moment, you were stuck in one place in time.

The key to managing expectations is **_not to have expectations._** Instead, let time do its thing without expectation. Now, this may seem farfetched, but give it a moment and read on.

Many times, people tend to label their time as good or bad. Why not just consider what happens as something that is or is not? Spending time with someone or with something with pre-set expectations is not a good idea. The reason for this is the emotions accompanying the label of a "bad time." Simply put, the time spent with someone or something should be unjudged. Consider this…

If a person wins a game, does that mean he had a good time? Alternatively, if he did not win the game, it was "bad" time spent? Not necessarily. If the person who lost the game had loads of fun and enjoyed themselves can consider the time spent "fun." Labeling time as 'bad' unnecessarily invokes negative emotions and takes away the positive emotions from the good portion of the time spent playing the game.

The technique of managing expectations takes place mentally and emotionally. Human beings tend to react to situations and circumstances almost entirely automatically. Our reaction to an unmet expectation is usually negative. We all know that negative energy drains a person mentally and emotionally, and when a person is drained, their attitude becomes sour, and so does the rest of their day. All this can be avoided by dealing with unmet expectations differently and not automatically.

Dealing with unmet expectations takes a willingness to be intentional. So, take a moment and reflect on your life's situations and circumstances. Was there ever a time when an unmet expectation made you angry and upset? How did you feel at that moment?

Feelings of anger and frustration during times when we wanted something to happen and it didn't, or times when something we did not want to happen but did happen, do not change what did or did not happen. For example, a girl expected her partner to ask for marriage after dating for a year but he didn't propose. Or we somehow got into a traffic (fender bender) accident, and wished it did not happen. It is natural to react with anger and frustration in both situations and circumstances. But, when using the technique of managing expectations, there is no automatic reaction to either of these cases.

Managing expectations requires you to hold your instinctual reaction and instead intentionally look at the brighter side. In the case of no marriage proposal, the couple gets more time to get to know each other with a firmer foundational friendship. In the case of the traffic accident, your car was not severely damaged, and no one got hurt. See how with intentionality and a bit of disciplining of one's emotions and mentality, it is possible to be positive in moments of distress or disappointment? It is an intentional technique of reframing the situation and circumstances to look at them in a more positive light.

It takes a great deal of focus and concentration in addition to intentionality to overcome times when things seemingly go wrong and fail to meet expectations. Focus and concentration are the same as mindfulness to reframe the situation. Taking a situation of disappointment and reframing it with deliberation to see its benefit lessens the stress and strain that usually occurs when things don't go as planned.

Now consider this scenario.

Jim and Anne took a ten-day cruise from Seattle, Washington, to Juneau, Alaska, and back to Seattle. One might consider this event to be fun since it was a cruise, right? On the first five days of the cruise, all was glorious. The food was delicious, the crew was terrific, and the scenery was spectacular. But on the sixth day, the ship's crew and some passengers got sick, so the cruise was cut short in Skagway, Alaska. On the seventh day of the ten-day cruise, they were airlifted back to Seattle and given a voucher for another cruise at the rate paid for the cruise cut short. Now, would this cruise experience be considered good or bad?

Implementing the trick of managing expectations says this experience was as it was. The food, crew, and scenery were incredible. Getting cut short of three days did not change the fact that the food, staff, and view were awesome. While it was unfortunate that the cruise was cut short, brooding over the lost three days is a waste of time. So, rather than spending time brooding over the incident and labeling it as a bad experience because of the lost three days, Jim and Anne can recognize the event as is and can choose to move onward with positive emotions and thoughts. To do otherwise is to waste time and energy.

You must be thinking that managing expectations takes too much time and effort, right? Well, you are not wrong. Managing expectations involves intentionality, focus, and discipline. *Without the intention and discipline to manage expectations, a person does not control what happens in the day; what happens in the day controls the person.* Rather than becoming a victim of circumstances, how about having control over the fallout of circumstances? We cannot control external situations and circumstances, but we can control how we react to them. As you can see from this example, how we respond to the conditions and circumstances can eat up our time in the day if we allow it. We can ensure that time is not wasted on negative emotions that do not change anything that has happened; in some cases, adverse reactions can make situations worse and take away even more time.

Cynthia Bazin stated that among the eight things successful people do is not get involved in "emotionally draining activities." She said, "If you want to step into a truly successful life, you have to focus on the things that positively fuel your life."[10] It is a waste of time lamenting the loss of three days. Not to mention that this lamentation could overshadow the food's, crew's, and scenery's awesomeness. So, managing expectations in this way makes it possible not to waste time or be stressed and miss out on the good times.

Exerting energy grunting over situations that are out of your control is a waste of time. Here's another scenario that challenges people to reframe a situation of less liking.

John, an architect, and Mary, an interior decorator plan to have their own home constructed from the ground up on a five-acre lot they purchased two years ago. They want to build their home with customized blueprints and their own home designs for inside and outside. After several months, they find the company they feel the most comfortable with for working with them to build their home.

It takes two months to draw up the architectural blueprints for the building of the house. They also decide on a budget for the project. Mary looks forward to designing the interior of the

---

10. Bazin, Cynthia (2014) 8 Things Successful People Never Waste Time Doing. Success. Retrieved from www.success.com

house with a portion of the budget as planned. John and Mary are confident that within six months, the house will be built, and they can start finishing the inside with decorations and furnishings. However, during the building of the house, the cost of the building materials increases in the third month and this puts a strain on the agreed budget. Now a project this big has a lot at stake and under these circumstances, knowing the project is not going as planned results in a lot of stress too. Normally, this would cause people to lose sleep and lose confidence in the project. However, since John and Mary know the benefit of being positive, they approach this situation as an opportunity and challenge.

John and Mary meet with the contractor and begin analyzing the building plan and blueprint, looking for ways to modify the original agreement to fit with the new budget. This takes time and energy, but it is done with positivity. They create a new building plan that fits with the budget of the project to the satisfaction of John and Mary. It turns out that with this modification, they can get more living space in certain areas of the house, and in doing so, there is greater enjoyment in what the interior will look and feel like after it is built and furnished.

Approaching this circumstance with positivity lessened the stress, allowed clearer thinking, and was froth with creativity in meeting the challenge together head-on. Reframing a bummer situation into a possible blessing circumstance is what John and Mary did and as a result, their home became more spacious and, in the end, more to their liking.

Are you beginning to see how reframing a situation that would normally be considered a bummer becomes a blessing?

Author's Anecdote

I spent most of my life judging how things went or did not go as expected. This behavior was instilled in me while growing up and I thought this is how a person is supposed to live. But one day, after experiencing too many disappointments, I began wondering if there was a better way to look at life and live each moment of the day. To help with this, I read the book "The Power of Positive Thinking" by Norman Vincent Peale, which confirmed that there was a better way to look at life and live it with less stress and decided to conduct an experiment. For one month, with intentionality and discipline, I guarded myself against automatically reacting to unmet expectations or unexpected occurrences. Admittedly, it took several restarts to the experiment. However, during the experiment, there were a full 30 days of living with positivity and not reacting to situations and circumstances with automatic negative emotions and negative thoughts.

The exciting thing during the 30-day experiment was fewer days of feeling tired and drained. Another result was feeling less harmful and more positive. Before, I felt negative, and a heaviness in my chest all the time. Soon, after the experiment, I took significant efforts to follow the new mindset with intentionality and discipline. After about three months, I automatically started approaching situations and circumstances with positivity and no expectations.

The best way to approach this technique is to consider it as something reframed. When you reframe an incident, you are essentially spinning it in a positive light. In the case of the cruise, the negative occurrence was reframed to a positive outcome. The same goes for the negative circumstances surrounding unmet expectations. Perhaps not having expectations gave way to having more time for a greater positive experience when what is expected eventually occurs. Choosing to reframe a situation or circumstance takes intention. Most people that reframe incidents do so with ease eventually, but at first, it takes practice. The best part is that when you do this repeatedly, you will find yourself feeling more satisfied with life, less stressed, and more positive in general.

Discussion Questions

1. When something does not go as planned, what thoughts come to your mind?

2. When something does not happen as you would have liked, how does that make you feel?

3. How do you normally react to circumstances and situations that don't go as planned or expected?

4. What thoughts come to mind when learning about a new way of handling unplanned and unexpected moments?

Quiz

━━

1. **A trick to use for being in control of time is _____.**

   a. monitoring moments in the day

   b. managing expectations

   c. managing emotions

2. **Managing expectations actually involves _____.**

   a. intentionality

   b. willingness

   c. attitude

3. **Humans tend to react to situations and circumstances _____.**

   a. positively

   b. neutrally

   c. negatively

4. **You feel drained when _____.**

   a. your expectations are not met

   b. you react negatively to unmet expectations

   c. expected things happen

5. **People who react negatively to situations feel a heaviness.**

   a. True

   b. False

6. **Reacting negatively to unmet expectations leads to _____.**

   a. wasted time and energy

   b. feeling tired

   c. both answers are correct

7. **Managing expectations is a technique used to _____.**

   a. avoid wasting time and energy

   b. feel less angry

   c. none of these answers are correct

8. **Situations and circumstances are often _____.**

   a. within our control

   b. out of our control

   c. something we automatically react to negatively

9. **It is more natural to react _____ to unmet expectations.**

   a. negatively

   b. positively

   c. neutral

10. It only takes intentionality to manage expectations.

    a. True

    b. False

Answers	1 – b	2 – a	3 – c	4 – b	5 – a
	6 – c	7 – a	8 – c	9 – a	10 – b

Chapter Summary

◆ Managing expectations does not come naturally.

◆ Humans tend to react to situations and circumstances negatively.

◆ It takes intentionality and discipline to guard against reacting negatively to situations and circumstances.

◆ It is possible to not pass judgment on everything that happens, and by doing that we don't waste time or energy lamenting over something that is not in our control.

◆ Living a life of having no expectations saves time and energy and allows for a lifetime of lightness and not having the feeling of heaviness.

This page is intentionally left blank

Chapter 4

Techniques for Finding the Time When Time is Lost

Key learning objectives should include the readers' understanding of the following:

- How monitoring and managing time helps with finding the time that was lost

- How finding lost time enables you to gain time in the future

- How to manage and monitor where the time is spent as a remote worker

- How applying wisdom and understanding prevent loss or waste of time

- How to preserve and protect your relationships and reputation

Have you ever felt tired at seven o'clock in the evening and asked yourself, "where did the time go?" Feeling tired and worn out from what? (you ask) The day was spent somehow but you don't feel satisfied. Instead, you're wondering how the time was spent and whether or not anything got accomplished in the day.

This happens when intentionality and productivity are not in play—the clock ticks by without notice of what is occurring. However, when managing time using the technique of intentionality and productivity, it is possible to find the time that was lost. Consider this scenario.

Jack and Jill intend to visit their parents next holiday season in Spain. There are three months left to plan the trip. In the first month, they discuss about plane tickets, rental cars, and purchasing gifts. Two months go by, and there is still talk of taking this trip, but no plane ticket has been purchased, rental car reservation made, and no one has visited the stores either online or onsite to purchase gifts. Now, there are only two weeks remaining for the date they decided to take the trip but the ticket prices have skyrocketed, there are no rental cars available, and taking this trip is no longer feasible.

It is plain to see that time slipped away without intentionality and productivity or with the use of working backward in time. One way that Jack and Jill can get back the lost time is to take the loss of time and turn it into a lesson for the next holiday season. Moment by moment, plan after plan, it is possible to regain the time lost by changing how time is used.. Amy Ormon stated, "You can't make up for the lost time. You can only do better in the future."[11]

At the very least, two months in advance, the plane tickets should have been bought, and the rental car reservation made.

---

11. Finn, Amy (2022) 140 Time Quotes on Making Every Second Count. *Quote Ambition*. Retrieved from www.quoteambition.com

This action follows the intentionality and productivity technique and tricks and works well using the working backward technique.

Time lost is the same as time wasted. Remember, the intention of this book is for you to not waste or lose time. So, when you feel like time is lost, that is the time to look for how and when it was lost to prevent this from happening again.

Finding the lost time can be tricky; however, the more you do this, the more you begin to realize the value of working backward with intentionality and discipline and managing expectations. So, let's rewind the clock a bit on the scenario with Jack and Jill.

Jack and Jill could have worked backward to avoid the purchase of a high-cost ticket, missing the availability of car rentals, and losing the chance of taking this trip to see their parents.

Let's use the matrix from Chapter 1 to see what can be done to find the time that was lost for next time!

Table 4.1   Working Backward Chart For Preparing and Planning to Visit Parents

Event	(What is the event?)	Family visit to Spain
Date of the event	(When is the event taking place)	December 20-30
Reason or purpose of the event	(What is the reason or purpose of the event?)	Want to visit parents
Things needed for the event	(What things do you need for the event?)	Plane tickets Rental car Gift item Money for gas, taking parents out to eat, and recreation while visiting Insurance for the rental car

Tasks that need to be done	Resources to get the task done	Deadline to complete
Research the types of airfares available and from what carriers	Internet	August 1
Research the types and cost of rental cars	Internet	August 1
Purchase plane tickets	Airline website	August 1
Make a car rental reservation.	Car rental website	August 1
Research recreation destinations and the cost of them	Internet	October 20
Purchase gift items for parents	Online or in the store	December 1
Pack suitcases		December 19

Now that the matrix is completed and intentionality was followed through with productivity, it is possible for Jack and Jill to save money on the airfare, reserve a rental car, and have a pleasant visit with their parents.

How much time do you suppose it took to sit down and complete the matrix? Do you see how much less anguish and less stress was experienced from taking the time to complete this matrix? Are you beginning to see just how much control we have over our time?

As stated in Chapter 3, external situations and circumstances are beyond our control, but how we react to them is within our control. Consider this as you realize the value of working backward with intentionality and discipline. Internal situations and circumstances can and must be controlled.

Using the working backward matrix makes it possible to work backward and be totally prepared for what is about to take place in one's life. This type of control is liberating. You are not a victim of what takes place in time; you are the master. The moments in a day are yours to determine which way they go.

You become the master of the moments in your day when working backward. You also control the use of the time and ensure there is no waste of time, no embarrassing moments, and, most important of all, no regrets.

However, when you realize time has been lost, how do you go about finding it?

Working backward and retracing your steps is how you can see where time was lost. When you determine what happened at the point when the time was lost, you learn what should've been done instead.

Recovering lost time in the case of a relationship makes people realize what it takes to have a smoother relationship. Taking the time to determine what action steps should be taken is a great way to preserve, protect and keep the relationship growing closer and moving forward.

For example, there may have been a time when your partner needed you to help them with the household chores but you did not do it. This caused a moment of discord, derision, and stress in the relationship. Being aware of the consequences of failing to follow through with a request such as this is what intentionality and discipline are all about. This way, there is no wasted time and energy on an unmet expectation that is in your control. You see the time that was lost and recover the lost time for the next time a request is made of you.

Ensuring relationships don't fall apart is important. Still, another good reason for being aware of what you do with your time is to prevent moments of embarrassment, ridicule, and regret.

Ever shown up to an event unprepared? If yes, you may have had plenty of time to ensure that you were ready to do your part as expected and obligated to do, yet, when the event occurred, you came up short. In cases like these, you fail to meet expectations and obligations, your credibility diminishes, and you have to face moments of. In such moments, questions like "why wasn't I better prepared?" "where did I waste my time that I could've used to be better prepared?" or "why did I fail to do what was needed to be prepared?" come to mind. Rest assured; you are not alone in having moments like these.

Millions of people have experienced moments where they had plenty of time to prepare for an event or participate in a project but when the time came, they could not do their part as expected.

For example, if you were to participate in a sports competition but were missing a piece of sports equipment, such as your shin guards, you would not be able to participate in the competition. If you had to give a sales presentation but forgot the thumb drive that had the pitch deck at home, you would not be able to give the presentation as planned. In both these cases, you come up short, face ridicule, and embarrassment, and could even be dismissed from the soccer team or the sales team. Needless to say, in moments like these, you ask yourself what went wrong when you came to the game or the presentation unprepared. It's simple. You lost time.

To prevent losing track of the time which can cause moments of embarrassment and regret, it is best to use the technique of intentionality with productivity and working backward to ensure that you are fully prepared for the event.

Maybe you need more convincing that taking the time to complete this matrix with intentionality and discipline is the way to go. Read this author's anecdote.

Author's Anecdote

There was a time when I was the same as most people and wasted time during the day. I would not plan for anything and approached each day without any plan, flying by the seat of my pants. Doing that caught up with me at a critical moment in time. Here is what happened.

My job responsibility grew to the point where I supervised others in completing the team's mission. The mission goals meant that each team member performed to their utmost effort and ability, and it was my job to see that this happened. There was no preplanning for completing this mission; consequently, it was not completed as needed. The mission goals were such that not meeting them adversely affected the whole organization. There was much adverse reaction throughout the organization, and I and the team faced ridicule, shame, and extreme embarrassment. If that was not punishment enough, I and my team were fired.

This experience led me to introspect about what went wrong and how to prevent that from happening in the future. Essentially, this was the first time I looked for lost time in my life. I started looking in the past to work backward in the future. I began being more intentional with using time, not just for myself but for others too.

In time, I was hired to supervise a team with the mission, goals, and objectives directed by my superiors. Having learned a hard lesson from the past, I approached this new team's mission with intentionality, productivity, and discipline, leading the others on the team to do the same thing. This time, the result was very different than in the past. The team performed superbly and accomplished the goals and objectives, which delighted the superiors and the organization's members.

Life lessons such as these reinforce the need to master the use of time and not allow time to slip away, be lost, and be wasted. Ensuring all the items needed for an event, project, or mission are in hand ensures a more positive outcome. Working backward with intentionality and discipline, managing expectations, and monitoring moments gives less stress, boosts productivity, and churns out positive results every day and in every situation and circumstance.

Looking back to discover where time was lost is the same thing as finding where the time was lost and being wiser for the future. By using this technique, you will know how to plan and prepare for the next event, or the next time your boss assigns you, or you and your team a work task. This time, you will be totally ready and prepared to be your best self and do your best with no loss of time, disappointment, or regret.

Discussion Questions

1. Discuss about a time in your life when if you could, you would rewind time

2. Have you ever wanted a "do-over" in your lifetime? If yes, why?

3. Recall an incident when you felt like a victim of something that happened that you might have been able to control.

Quiz

1. To get back time that is lost is to _____.

    a. to call for it to come to you

    b. to wish it was never lost

    c. turn the lost time into a lesson for the future

2. Moment by moment, plan after plan it is possible to regain the time lost by changing how time is used.

    a. True

    b. False

3. When you examine a plan that went awry, you _____.

    a. discover what happened at the time

    b. discover what could have been done to preserve time.

    c. both answers are correct

4. Time lost is the same thing as time _____.

    a. discovered

    b. wasted

    c. gone forever

5. **It is possible to ensure that future events go as planned by reflecting on past mistakes.**

    a. True

    b. False

6. **Learning from _____ helps to experience more positive and less negative situations.**

    a. watching others

    b. past mistakes

    c. research

7. **With the use of the _____, it is possible to work backward and be prepared for what is about to take place in one's life.**

    a. matrix

    b. sounding board

    c. calendar

8. **You become the _____ of the moments in your day when working backward.**

    a. master

    b. victim

    c. victor

9. **External situations and circumstances are beyond our control, but how we react to them is within our control.**

    a. True

    b. False

10. **The time that was lost is often due to _____.**

    a. not monitoring moments in the day

    b. failing to preplan

    c. not working backward

Answers	1 – c	2 – a	3 – c	4 – b	5 – a
	6 – b	7 – a	8 – a	9 – a	10 – c

Chapter Summary

◆ It is possible to find the time that is lost.

◆ The more you probe into the time lost in the past, the less time you lose in the future.

◆ Learning from the past helps to experience more positive outcomes in the future.

Part 2: Time Management for the Remote Worker

There is a different dynamic to working at home and different factors connected to this type of work environment, unlike working onsite. For example, distractions that can cause a waste of time if not handled properly can take away the effort and energy of being productive. This chapter addresses the issues that arise from working at home and provides guidance with tips, tricks, and techniques for protecting work time and improving work performance.

Key learning objectives should include the reader's understanding of the following:

- How flexibility and work/life balance can be maximized for both home and work productivity

- How to manage distractions

- How to manage and monitor where the time is spent as a remote worker

- How to remain in control of the time each day

- How to preserve and protect your work image and the quality of your work

Remote workers have a different working arrangement than workers who work onsite. Remote workers perform their work tasks at a distance from where their employer is based and are trusted to use their time wisely. The remote worker's time is often highly regulated or not regulated at all, and they work autonomously. When remote workers work autonomously, they are responsible for using their time productively. Producing deliverables is the one actual evidence that the remote worker is using their time wisely. That is evident to both the employer and employee, but what takes place behind the scenes to make this happen is not apparent. To deliver excellent results, the remote worker needs to use his/her time wisely. Knowing how to spend time working at home while managing distractions (voluntary and involuntary timewasters) makes the remote working experience something to enjoy and not have to endure.

Chapter **5**

Tips for Mastering Time in the Day

Working remotely requires a tremendous amount of trust and confidence on the employer's part. As such, it becomes essential to make each minute count, responsibly. To that end, the remote employee must account for what they do during their work session. Not only that, but due to the flexibility and work/life balance that comes with working at home, there is a way to master each moment to the remote employee's and online employer's greater satisfaction. That method is to make a list and check it twice, literally.

Key learning objectives should include the reader's understanding of the following:

- How to always know where the time is spent as a remote worker and have extra time in the day

- How to successfully use time blocking to fit in the home and work tasks and obligations

- How to muster intentionality to manifest set goals for work, home, and yourself

- How to have a life of fulfilled promises using the time-blocking method successfully

5.1 Make a List and Check it Twice

Minutes of the work session that is not regulated must be autonomously and responsibly held by you as a remote employee. There is an element of trust that you will carry out your job responsibilities to the best of your ability and without fail. The trust factor is increased every time you come through with a completed task for your online employer. The best and easiest way to be consistent with completing your tasks and giving the best results is to write down the deliverables for the day.

Consider this scenario. You are an insurance adjuster working from home. In this case, you have an onsite portion of the job that must be scheduled. You write the damage reports in your car by which the insurance claim is adjusted and paid in the car. You, a Claims Adjuster, communicate with your online employer via their home computer and complete time sheets, mileage sheets, and time off requests, all from your home-based office. This is why this remote job category is called **working from home.** However, **working at home** refers to a remote worker who does 100% of the job tasks from their home computer, not leaving the house. There is a distinction and a different work dynamic between working at home and working from home. In the case of an insurance adjuster who does most of the job tasks outside the home, it is working from home.

Time-blocking is intentionally dividing the time of the day into blocks assigned to a specific task, action, or activity. Using a time block method, the tasks for the job and tasks for the household are listed in time blocks. Working with this method takes intentionality, prioritizing, discipline, and flexibility. The time it takes to complete the job tasks may override the home tasks, and therefore, you need to prioritize and have flexibility in accomplishing the home tasks. Naturally, you have to act responsibly for completing the job tasks as they take the top priority. However, given that the claims adjustment appointment usually lasts only one hour, it is possible to squeeze in home tasks. But, whenever the job task takes longer than usual, it is possible that you cannot complete your home task.

On the time-blocking list for you as an Insurance Claims Adjuster is the location of the vehicle, distance, time to be at the vehicle location, and approximate arrival and departure time. Next on the list are errands, such as stopping at the grocery store, picking up dry cleaning, taking a walk in the park, visiting a sick friend, or stopping at the school and having lunch with your child.

Here is an example of what this time blocking might look like for this scenario (starting the day at 8:00 am and ending at 5:30 pm):

Table 5.1   Time-blocking chart to accomplish work and home tasks in a day

Time of day	Work task	Home task
8:00 am travel to appointment #1	Claims adjustment (including the address of appointment, vehicle description for all appointment blocks)	
8:30 am	Claims adjustment appointment #1	
9:30 am		Pick up dry-cleaning (be sure to have the claim cheque)
10:30 am	Claims adjustment appointment #2	
12:00 pm		Lunch at school with child
1:30 pm	Claims adjustment appointment #3	
3:00 pm		Visit a sick friend /take a walk in the park
4:00 pm	Claims adjustment appointment #4	
5:30 pm		Stop at the store for groceries

In this scenario, the insurance adjuster does the job and has time to do an errand. Also on the list is the time it takes to write the report that gets sent to the office for processing within one hour of the claim's adjustment appointment. See how it is possible to fulfill a job and personal tasks? If the employer deliverables are submitted on time and with excellence, this scenario is possible. Repeating this type of list-making daily makes it possible to have a work life that is fulfilling for the employee, productive for the employer, and overall, a friendly and stress-free experience. But this kind of work experience can only take place if the job itself is not regulated.

In the case of a regulated work-at-home employment arrangement, such as working in a virtual call center, this kind of list-making and errand running is more challenging to accomplish. The virtual call center agent would need to communicate their time off with the team if possible. Most virtual call center work sessions are a straight eight hours with a small break in the morning and afternoon and a more extended break for lunch in between the morning and afternoon hours. Depending on where the errands take place to where the residence is located, it may be possible to fit in errands. But to do that, you need to use the intentionality technique. You need to form a list and have the discipline to follow through with what is on the list.

If you are working 100% with your computer at your home, you are **working at home.** It may be too that your work hours are scheduled and you have very little free time because they are highly regulated. If this is the case, your work time is regulated to the point where every minute is accounted for from the start of the work shift to the end. Even so, there is still a way to squeeze in home tasks on the scheduled breaks. In fact, it is strongly recommended that you use the time-blocking method to make the most of your break times to complete a task for the household.

Consider this scenario:

Susan is a travel agent working from her home office adjacent to the kitchen. She has a strict work session that begins at 9:00 am and ends at 5:00 pm with one hour lunch and two 15-minute breaks, one in the morning and one in the afternoon. Susan would like to accomplish the following tasks for her well-being and for the maintenance of the household: sweep the floor of the kitchen and the bathroom, vacuum the carpet in the living room and bedrooms, do one load of laundry, walk the dog, and write a letter to her sister. At this point, you may be thinking, "it is not possible to do all of this with a strict work session." Well, let's see about that with the time-blocking method.

Table 5.2	Time-blocking chart to accomplish work and home tasks within a day

Time of day	Work task	Home task
9:00 am	Start taking calls from travel clientele	
10:30 am	15-minute break	Put one load of laundry in the washing machine Sweep floor of the kitchen and the bathroom
10:45 am	Resume work session (taking calls from clients)	
12:30 pm	Lunch break	Eat lunch Move clothes to the dryer from washing machine Vacuum rug in the living room and bedrooms Write a letter (or start letter) to sister
1:30 pm	Resume work session taking calls from clients	
3:00 pm	15-minute break	Walk the dog
3:15 pm	Resume work session taking calls from clients	
5:30 pm	End work session	

For people who have regulated second shift work at home job positions, it is possible to make a list of errands to do before or after the shift, in the same way as someone who works outside the home. Likewise, the same is true for work-at-home employees that work the third shift. Make time to sleep and do errands intentionally. That means thinking and planning and making a list of errands before or after work makes it possible to have the obligations for work and home covered. Satisfying work and home obligations allow for a stress-free and more satisfying work experience, especially as a remote worker with freedom and flexibility.

5.2 Manage Moments by Making Them Count

Managing moments in the day takes intentionality and determination. Intentionality is a mental discipline, and determination is grit. It is more natural to just show up for the day, clock in, and take each moment as it comes. Most people live that way. I used to live that way too, but there were too many incidents where I unintentionally broke many promises. So, it became necessary to mix intention with determination to be more trustworthy and fulfill promises. In order to do that, it was necessary to keep track of the moments in the day and manage them so that all the job tasks, the ones for the employer and the ones for the house, were getting done in a timely manner and as promised. Time blocking is the one true method by which it is possible to take care of the professional and personal life simultaneously.

Going back to the scenario of an insurance adjuster, it is easier to see how this technique operates and makes a difference.

Consider this scenario. You (an insurance adjuster) also have a set financial and time budget. The terms of the position include the management of the financial budget, making sure not to go over the allotted amount for gasoline, food, and car repairs for travel to the location where the damage may have occurred. The employer is only dictating the budget for expenses. But if you want to cover the basis for meeting work and home obligations, there is another budget to manage; that budget is time.

In this scenario, you must visit no less than five locations where there is damage, and the persons make an insurance claim. The locations and the expense involved must be planned out, as well as the time it takes to arrive, do the inspection, and return home.

There needs to be intentionality and determination to manage the moments along with the expenses. The intention is to not go over the expense budget and to be determined to make excellent use of the moments in the day. Writing down the location and distance to get there is the first step. The next step is to write down the errand, the site, and the distance, and be determined to be disciplined.

On Monday, you promise your child to meet for lunch at school on Tuesday. The lunchtime in the school is noon. Two insurance claim inspections on Tuesday will be done before the school lunch. It takes one hour to reach each location and thirty minutes of travel time. In addition, you also want to visit a friend in the hospital which is a thirty-minute drive from the residence and thirty minutes away from the first inspection location. The second inspection location is thirty minutes from the school location. Starting from home at 8:00 am makes it possible to travel to the inspection locations, visit a sick friend, and go to the school for lunch.

Here's what the time-blocking would look like for this scenario:

Table 5.3	**Time-blocking chart to accomplish work and home tasks**

Time of day	Work task	Home task
8:00 am – 8:30 am	Travel to Appointment #1	
8:30 am – 9: 30 am	Complete Appointment #1	
9:30 am-10:00 am		Travel to the hospital to visit the sick friend
10:00 am – 10:30 am		Visit with sick friend
10:30 am - 11:00 am	Travel to Appointment #2	
11:00 am – 12:00 noon	Complete Appointment #3	
12:00 pm – 12:30 pm	Travel to school	
12:30 pm – 1:00 pm		Eat lunch with child
1:00 pm – 1:30 pm	Travel to Appointment #4	
1:30 pm – 2:30 pm	Complete Appointment #4	
2:30 pm – 3:00 pm	Travel to Appointment #5	
3:00 pm – 4:00 pm	Complete Appointment #5	
4:00 pm – 4:30 pm	Travel back to residence -location of home office	
4:30 pm – 5:00 pm	Complete the daily report and email to boss	

What do you suppose might have happened if you did not act with intention, determination, and with discipline? You guessed it. The school lunch date might have been missed or, at the very least, you would have shown up late. Not to mention feeling bad and very stressed over the unfulfilled promise to the child and perhaps to the sick friend. Acting with intention, by making a list, checking it twice, and following through with the intention using determination and discipline makes it possible to work with integrity, and fulfill all obligations efficiently and effectively.

Determination is the mentality of wanting to do something, and discipline is a mechanism by which you want to get it done. It's one thing to write down in a matrix what needs to be done for work and home, it's quite another thing when what is written down is manifested.

Manifesting what tasks need to be accomplished can only happen through planning, preparing, and then persevering with determination and discipline. After using this method and experiencing the joy of fulfilling promises and meeting expectations (from your boss, family members, friends, teachers, community members, pets, etc.), you will begin to feel and sense the logic in using this method to master the moments in the day.

Mastering the moments in the day can only be effectively done using the time-blocking method for the day. Whether you are a regulated remote worker or a non-regulated and completely autonomous worker, it is possible to do your household tasks during work hours. It takes planning using the time-blocking method. As you can see from the examples of the scenarios, it is possible to squeeze together work and home tasks on the same day.

Still need a bit more convincing to use the time-blocking method for mastering moments in your day? Read this author's anecdote.

Author's Anecdote

There was a time when I let the events of the day dictate what took place and did not take control of the time in my day. One incident that comes to mind is when my oldest child had a special event taking place at school and I was expected to attend it. It was put on the calendar, and I even assured my child that I would be there. My oldest child got on the school bus feeling great that his mom would be attending this special event. But, back then, I was not aware of the time-blocking method of mastering time in the day and as a result, missed attending this special school event. Needless to say, my oldest son's feelings were hurt, and it took a very long time to heal those emotional wounds.

Without discipline and determination, an event written on the calendar can easily be missed, unintentionally.

There were several more instances such as this when promises were broken due to not paying attention to the time. Then one day, I decided to start taking stock of the situation. Since I was sincere in making the promise but was lacking a way of knowing how to fulfill the promise, I sought advice from friends who looked like they had more control over their lives than I did at that time. These friends were the ones who introduced me to mastering time in the day using the time-blocking method.

Admittedly, at first, it was hard to use this method because it demanded discipline along with

> determination. After mustering the determination and diligently practicing this method, it was long before the results were realized. Not missing events, fulfilling promises, and even having more time left in the day to spend with leisure gave me more determination and discipline to use this method. With more practice, I mastered this method and can now juggle many things in a day successfully and fulfill my promises.

At first, time blocking will feel weird and take a lot of energy and effort. But the more you do it, the easier it gets. You begin experiencing the benefits of using this method almost instantly. All of a sudden, you will notice that your stress level is reduced, people in your life are trusting you more, and there are moments in the day you can use for leisure. You have a lot to look forward to when using the time-blocking method.

Discussion Questions

1. How many times in your life did you promise to do something, but time flew away and the promise was unfulfilled?

2. Picture yourself living a life of fulfilled promises. What does that look like?

Quiz

1. Monitoring the _____ in the day takes place intentionally and watchfully, making sure the time spent is productive to accomplishing goals.

    a. events

    b. time

    c. moments

2. This is a mental discipline with grit.

    a. Intentionality

    b. Determination

    c. Diligence

3. For the remote employee, there is an element of _____ that the remote employee will perform their job responsibilities to the best of their ability, without fail.

    a. respect

    b. positivity

    c. trust

4. _____ is the mentality of wanting to do something, and _____ is a mechanism by which one can get it done.

   a. Domination, determination

   b. Determination, discipline

   c. Discipline, determination

5. The _____ factor is increased every time the remote employee comes through with the completed task for the online employer.

   a. respect

   b. trust

   c. positivity

6. Managing moments in the day takes _____ and _____.

   a. intentionality, determination

   b. willpower, way power

   c. grit, determination

7. It is not possible to manage personal and professional tasks on the same day.

   a. True

   b. False

8. Time blocking takes _____ at first when doing it to manage moments in the day.

   a. time

   b. energy

   c. grit

9. Mastering the moments in the day can only be effectively done using the _____ method.

   a. time

   b. monitoring

   c. time blocking

10. Acting with intention, by making a list, checking it twice, and following through with the intention using determination and discipline makes it possible to work with integrity, and fulfill all obligations efficiently and effectively.

   a. True

   b. False

Answers	1 – c	2 – b	3 – c	4 – b	5 – b
	6 – a	7 – b	8 – b	9 – c	10 – a

Chapter Summary

◆ It is possible to accomplish home tasks and job tasks simultaneously.

◆ Using the time-blocking method, it is possible to see the tasks that need to be done and the time by which they need to be done.

◆ By using determination and discipline, it is possible to follow the plan to get the tasks done in accordance with the time blocked.

◆ Results from using this method are less stress, more trust built, and more fulfilled promises.

Chapter 6

Tricks to Use for Being in Control of Time

There are moments in all human lives when controlling time does not seem possible. When dependent on the actions of others or when the time is regulated are two scenarios where we cannot intentionally control time. But except for these two scenarios, it is possible to have control of time and to make it count. In cases such as these, there is a special way by which this is done effectively, and the special way is to manage others' expectations.

Key learning objectives should include the reader's understanding of the following:

- How to always be in control of time planned, prepared, and spent for remote work and home life

- How to manage expectations of your boss and household successfully

- How to identify lost time to gain time for the future

- How to avoid embarrassing (and potentially career-ending) moments at work using the P.A.U.S.E. method

6.1 Manage Expectations

Unlike the managing of one's own expectations, this section discusses the management of others' expectations. This is when you promise to do something by a certain time, and something happens that causes you to fail in the fulfillment of the promise. Consider this scenario to see how this is done.

Joseph, a remote worker, promises his supervisor to research and report the findings regarding some data statistics, which the supervisor needs to report to their supervisor. The promise is made, the research is done and the report is written by the end of the week. But, something occurs that prevents Joseph from fulfilling this promise. To manage expectations properly and effectively, with all due respect, Joseph communicates this unfulfillment the moment the obstacle is seen as a hindrance to completing this research and report.

Do not waste any time telling the supervisor. To stay stress-free and have a blissful working relationship, any hindrance must be communicated the moment it is known to you. This way, the supervisor can ask someone else and still get what's needed for reporting to their supervisor. This is managing expectations effectively and with respect.

Of course, the better scenario is to fulfill the promise and not need to communicate a hindrance, but life happens. Remember, in the case of a hindrance or distraction keeping you from producing an expected deliverable, most especially as a remote employee, you must preserve trust and immediately communicate the situation to your supervisor.

Managing expectations is a sure way to maintain the trust factor that is vital for the remote employee and online employer's relationship. We all know what happens when trust in a relationship is broken. Not fulfilling the expectations of an online employer definitely leads to a break in trust, which potentially can cause the relationship to break apart. And a broken employment relationship may lead to unemployment. So, it behooves the remote employee to make sure their deliverables are met as expected by their online employer, or that any delay in completing a task is communicated in advance.

It goes without saying that too many times when an expected deliverable is not delivered on time, it leads to a situation whereby the online employer will no longer accept tardiness of delivery. So, let's examine one factor that could possibly hinder remote employees from fulfilling their work obligations on time. One thing that remote workers deal with more than their counterparts working in the same physical space is distractions at home.

6.2 Manage Distractions

It is very uncomfortable for most humans to have to admit not living up to a promise, especially when the promise was made to a manager of an online employer. In this case, one might want to observe what may have caused this unfulfilled promise to the manager. For remote employees, the cause is often due to distractions.

Managing distractions takes intentionality, determination, and vigilance. Distractions such as noise, children or pets vying for attention, the doorbell, the cell phone, the radio, or even the sound of the neighbor mowing the lawn can adversely affect concentration. We all know the outcome of our distracted minds. We can miss placing punctuation in a paragraph correctly, misspell someone's name, dial the wrong number, type in the wrong code, or worse --- send a personal text to someone on the leadership team by mistake. A diverted mind that takes away our ability to be accurate is a recipe for disaster. Having to deal with distractions comes with the territory of working remotely. But, it is possible to work remotely with few distractions and not risk a loss of family relationships or friendships.

Consider this scenario.

Single mother of three children, ages 7, 9, and 14, works for an online employer as a project manager. Her job is to manage three major construction projects and have weekly update reports submitted by 4:00 pm every Friday. For the most part, this mother does a great job coordinating these projects and submitting the reports on time. But during one of the weeks, two of the children get measles and are at home. She is used to working with all three children in school and there are no distractions. But this particular week, having the two children home is a distraction, and she falls behind in her work. What should she do?

Managing distractions in this scenario is to communicate with her children in advance when she starts work for the day and the times she is available for them. She can say, "I will be in my office from 9 am to 12 noon and will check in with you at noon." By saying this, she assures her children that she will check up on them after some time, and the power of the distraction is diminished. By communicating her availability, she maintains the relationship with her children, as well as the ability to work with excellence.

This is one of the hundreds of other cases by which a remote employee, to minimize work distractions, must act with intentionality, determination, and vigilance. Once again, it is the responsibility of the remote employee to manage their work environment to protect it against anything that can hinder work and to preserve and protect time from being lost.

Consider the below situation and see what you would do in this case.

An elderly parent is dependent on you for everything: shopping, cleaning the house, doing the laundry, paying the bills, using the bathroom, bathing, and making sure they maintain a healthy diet and healthy attitude. You work for an online employer as a data scientist in charge of building databases with tons of confidential data. Your weekly deliverable is to construct and maintain databases and run reports as needed by the company. This work takes a ton of concentration. There is no room for error. One error in any of the data fields could adversely affect the data outputs and skew the data reports the leadership of the company relies on for making top-level decisions.

One day, while working, your elderly parent sends a text message every ten minutes, hounding you about going shopping, constantly adding items to the shopping list. This has become a major distraction. What to do in this case?

The best way to handle this situation is to value their need for you to shop for them and validate their request with a timely reminder. Tell the elderly parent to set their alarm for 5:00 pm. When the alarm goes off, they can call you. In the meantime, take a piece of paper and write down what items come to mind for the shopping trip. See how making it clear when you are available stops this distraction? Now you can concentrate and get your job done correctly.

All it takes to manage distractions is intentionality, determination, and vigilance. There was intentional protection against losing concentration on the part of the mother with children home from school due to illness and in the case of the elderly parent. Managing time and protecting relationships takes intentionality and determination to follow through with what is promised and expected. In the case of the parent with children, the only way to do what needs to be done for work and home, and manage moments of distraction, is to be forthright and set boundaries. Managing expectations with those set boundaries occurred when giving the children the time of the parent's availability to clear a time pathway to work uninterrupted.

In the case of taking care of the elderly parent, it was necessary to set boundaries and help them manage those boundaries. It is challenging to keep elderly parents satisfied while having obligations for work, home, and other things. But, with discipline, determination, and understanding, it is possible.

Do you see how it is possible to manage distractions and protect yourself from losing focus and concentration? While it is possible to manage distractions, it is also possible to manage the outcome of having your focus and concentration interrupted at the moment of the distraction, using the P.A.U.S.E method.

6.3 P.A.U.S.E - Pulling Away Until Satisfied [Working] Excellently

Have you gotten into a hurry at work, at home, or at school and made a mistake that made you must redo your work? You are not alone! Over the years, I learned that one of the best ways to ensure time is not wasted is to never repeat your actions due to a mistake. One best way to do that is to pull away until satisfied that you are working excellently (P.A.U.S.E.). This takes discipline and intentionality and not waiting until the last minute. Procrastination puts a person in a situation of a hurry, and this is a big reason for making mistakes. Not only is time wasted, but your reputation for not doing excellent work may get destroyed by the mistakes you make.

You need to take a P.A.U.S.E. moment and use the technique of working backward from the deadline to save time from having to redo your work. Consider this scenario.

Jill must submit a business proposal on behalf of her company to the City Administrator by 4:00 pm Friday afternoon. It is 2:00 pm Tuesday afternoon as she looks at the clock. She is halfway done with typing up this proposal. Jill can procrastinate and pull an all-day and all-nighter on Thursday and Thursday evening in order to have this ready for someone to review on Friday morning, leaving very little time to make any changes. Or, she can say to herself, "I will do this by Thursday morning, so someone can review it, giving me plenty of time to make changes as needed."

By working on the proposal Tuesday afternoon and all day on Wednesday, she is less stressed and knows that there is plenty of time to get this done and have it reviewed before it is due to the City Administrator. Intentionally working with P.A.U.S.E. in her work ethic, Jill pauses before sending the proposal for just a moment while she makes sure there are no mistakes. She looks at the proposal draft after she completes it, reads it again, and notices some simple punctuation and spelling errors. Having taken a moment to P.A.U.S.E, she is now confident that she is submitting quality work to the reviewer.

Pausing to make sure that your work is excellent not only preserves and protects your work reputation, but it also saves you from wasting time. Pausing yourself before submitting the work is a great way to ensure less stress and more blissful days.

Looking over what you wrote, calculated, recommended, drew, and recorded in a moment of P.A.U.S.E. can save you from embarrassment, losing credibility, or even losing your job. As a remote worker at risk of losing concentration and focus during times when the distraction cannot be managed (such as a crying baby), using the P.A.U.S.E can save you. However, it does take discipline to stop yourself from sending the report, recording, drawing, analysis, etc. It also takes determination to ensure the work you produce is of high quality. When determining that, it becomes easy to pull yourself away from hitting the send button before you review the work. There is nothing wrong with having a trusted co-worker review it too. In fact, it is highly recommended you work with a buddy at work that you trust to review each other's work. As hard as we try, we tend to look at our own work with bias. Whereas someone else with their own lens can spot things we ourselves might miss.

Need a little more convincing to use P.A.U.S.E. in your workday? Consider this author's anecdote.

Author's Anecdote

There was a time when I worked at home as a corporate travel consultant arranging travel for high-level corporate clients. Taking calls from my bedroom's make-shift office, I handled hundreds of C-Level corporate clients' travel around the world. Normally, there would only be a 40-hour regulated work schedule, with high expectations for accuracy. For almost a year, all the reservations made were accurate and the corporate clients were delighted with the service rendered. However, there was a major hurricane that hit New York City hard and closed the three major international airports. There were fair warnings of this impending storm surge and the havoc it would wreak for the New Yorkers and for the people living close to the shoreline in New Jersey. Now imagine being an international traveler depending on the three major airports to travel internationally. Well, you can imagine that for the week of the hurricane and two weeks after, I, along with the other corporate travel consultants worked our fingers to the bone for extremely long days and nights to get our corporate traveler's home. Many of the corporate travelers were stuck overseas and needed immediate solutions for their plight.

Needless to say, in this storm emergency, there was extreme effort expended in getting our corporate clients rebooks and shuffled to other airports with shuttles to where they parked their cars. After working three weeks straight for 60-70 hours, some nights with only four hours of sleep, I committed a blunder with one of the corporate traveler's arrangements that cost the company thousands of dollars.

I wish I had learned the P.A.U.S.E. method so that I could have avoided this blunder. You see, another form of distraction is exhaustion. But, even in the state of exhaustion, taking a moment to see that the three-letter abbreviation on the plane reservation was incorrect would have saved the moment from becoming a disaster. You guessed it. The corporate client received the plane ticket for the wrong airport. The fallout from this mistake was terrible. My one-year employment contract had only two more weeks to go but ended two weeks early. All it would have taken was to P.A.U.S.E. and the mistake would have been caught, the correction made and the corporate traveler would have flown home with no problem. Instead, the company had to pay the difference it took to rebook the flights and make the correction to the travel arrangements for their CEO to make it home safe and sound.

Taking a P.A.U.S.E. averts disasters such as the one experienced by me as a corporate travel consultant. It can also ensure that you maintain high-quality work performance despite the tiredness, exhaustion, illness (even working with a fever could cause an error), and whatever else life throws at us and challenges our focus and concentration.

Discussion Questions

1. How many times have you found yourself late with turning in reports, recordings, analyses, drawings, or any other form of deliverable assigned and expected by your online employer?

2. Picture yourself never again turning in something full of mistakes. What does that look like?

3. Imagine all the time you save by not repeating your actions because you took the time to use the P.A.U.S.E. method. What does that look like?

Quiz

1. **Being in control of time and ensuring the quality of your work is excellent takes _____.**

    a. managing the expectations of the employer

    b. managing distractions

    c. both a and b

2. **Mastering the _____ of the day takes place intentionally with the way the time is spent.**

    a. events

    b. time

    c. moments

3. **All it takes to make things happen is to dream of them.**

    a. True

    b. False

4. **There is a trust factor in working remotely and the way time is spent is paramount to the continuance of that trust.**

    a. True

    b. False

5. **Manage moments by _____.**

   a. making them count

   b. counting the days

   c. keeping watch over the calendar

6. **Remote workers can keep the privilege of working remotely because they _____.**

   a. have the desire and discipline

   b. follow through with meeting deadlines and expectations

   c. have better attitudes than the ones working in the office

7. **An online employer must have the _____ and _____ in their remote employee for the working relationship to flourish.**

   a. trust, confidence

   b. intention, obligation

   c. inclination, patience

8. **Communicate _____ with the online employer when hindrances occur to preserve and protect the trust factor.**

   a. respectfully

   b. immediately

   c. woefully

9. **Remote workers with distraction must have the _____ to manage them.**

   a. determination

   b. discipline

   c. grit

10. **Pausing to make sure that your work is excellent not only preserves and protects your work reputation, but it also saves you from wasting time.**

    a. True

    b. False

Answers	1 – c	2 – c	3 – b	4 – a	5 – a
	6 – b	7 – a	8 – b	9 – a	10 – a

Chapter Summary

◆ Being a remote employee working for an online employer comes with expected deliverables.

◆ Managing expectations ensures that your credibility and trust with your online employer are intact.

◆ Managing distractions is possible as long as you have the intentionality, determination, and vigilance to do it.

◆ Distractions are manageable to the degree that it is possible to maintain good relationships with family and friends.

◆ Managing distractions ensure that the focus and concentration to do an excellent job are maintained and uninterrupted.

◆ Using P.A.U.S.E takes determination and discipline to protect the quality of your work and not make mistakes.

This page is intentionally left blank

Chapter **7**

Techniques for Finding the Time When Time is Lost

When you realize that time has been lost, that is the time to act immediately. Time lost, especially for a remote employee is not a good thing. An unfulfilled job task is an indication of lost time and we know all know what can happen if the job is not done properly. To prevent unfulfilled job tasks, it behooves the remote employee to learn and implement the technique of synchronicity with the work schedule.

Key learning objectives should include the reader's understanding of the following:

- How to avoid losing time and not fulfilling work obligations

- How to retrieve lost time and gain it for the future as a remote worker

- How to remain in control of the time each day so it does not slip away

> • How to preserve and protect your work image and family relationships

7.1 Observe Synchronicity With the Work Schedule

The term "synchronicity" was introduced by psychologist Carl Jung.[12] Synchronicity, in this context, is the intertwining of several events taking place within a short span of time. In the case of them being positive, they are all productive and fulfilling. In the case of them being negative (such as distractions), they are hindrances to productivity and fulfillment. Observing synchronicity with the work schedule means intentionally seeing the meaningful events taking place within the work session. These events can be positive or negative and elicit an appropriate response. In the case of the events being positive, the appropriate response would be to intentionally take action to continue the events. Conversely, if the events were negative ones, the appropriate response would be to take action to discontinue them. Consider the scenario.

A remote employee works as a virtual assistant and is married with two grown children. She gets up, makes breakfast for her and her husband and as her husband steps out of the door to go to his workplace 45 minutes away, she goes to her office in her bedroom from the kitchen. She logs into her computer and begins working on her tasks for her online employer. At 10:00 am she gets a call from one of her grown children and converses for about ten minutes and returns to her work tasks. At noon, she takes

---

12. www.carl-jung.net

an hour's break, eats lunch, and takes a walk in the park that is across the street from her house. At 1:00 pm she returns to doing her work tasks and at 3:00 pm she has a call with her supervisor lasting 15 minutes. At 4:30 pm, she logs out of her computer, returns to the kitchen, and prepares dinner for her husband who comes in at 5:00 pm.

See the synchronicity? She works on her tasks, talks to one of her children on call, and takes a walk. As a result, she is in a pleasant mood throughout the day. The events of both her professional and personal life take place synchronously. This did not just happen of its own volition. This synchronicity with the work schedule is deliberate and intentional and only possible since this virtual assistant is operating with intentionality and productivity. As such, the list of tasks for the employer is made, and the time for herself is built into the list, with plenty of time to take a call from her grown child. She experiences a pleasant and stress-free day due to this intentionality and productivity observed as synchronicity in her work schedule. Certainly, in this scenario, it is plain to see how the time of the day in the work schedule is being spent and how the spending of this time is leading to productivity and fulfillment. Now consider the scenario where the events taking place are negatively impacting the synchronicity of the work schedule.

John, a work-at-home career coach has a deliverable from the online employer to meet with thirty clients per week. Negative events taking place synchronously with the work schedule are thwarting the success of accomplishing this deliverable. Events such as family incivility, chronic pain, and obnoxious clients are getting in the way of performing the work to the satisfaction of both the remote employee and the online employer. In this case, the workday is full of stress, and this is evident when the career coach and the client interact. In this case, the negative events must be dealt with and cannot be ignored. Also, in this scenario, time is lost with the stress and strain because the career coach is attempting to work under stressful circumstances.

The synchronicity with the work schedule is disconcerting and must be handled one event at a time. Family incivility is a matter by which the family needs to rally and not revolt. Chronic pain must be dealt with with the help of medical professionals. Taking care of these two matters may just set a better tone for the interaction with the clients. In case it doesn't, then a simple chat with the client and with the employer should resolve that situation. In all three events, synchronous to the work schedule, stress is building and getting in the way of time spent well. By handling these negative events and eliminating them, it is possible to work with positive events such as in scenario 1.

Do you see how important it is to be observable of what is taking place with the work schedule? By doing so, you are preserving and protecting the time of the work schedule and making it less stressful, and more blissful.

7.2 Getting Back the Time That was Lost

Like the discussion in Chapter 4, time lost for remote workers is an opportunity to rectify their mistakes for the future. Knowing incidents that may occur that are time-wasting, distracting, and hindering to working with excellence is a great way to make sure to preserve and protect time. Observe them with the intention and determination to take action and do away with time wasters, objects and persons who are distractions, and things or situations that cause hindrances to completing the work as promised and expected.

Being present in body and mind is critical for having a high-quality work performance. If at the end of the work session, you see that not all the work tasks are getting done as they should, this may be an indicator that there is something getting in the way. Obviously, there is a time waster somewhere and it is a *must* that the time waster be identified and dealt with immediately.

You cannot afford to have a time waster that makes you lose time from completing a job task. There must be a way to see what may have happened that got in the way of working through a job task and then determine how to alleviate it.

For example, if you lost time from work due to phone calls, put your phone on silent or airplane mode until you are on a break from work. If the distraction is the sound of a lawnmower when your neighbor is mowing the lawn, close the windows or play soft music to keep from hearing the lawnmower. If the distraction is lack of sleep, then get a sleep test to see if you wake up from snoring and get a CPAP to get a good night's rest. Not dealing with the things that may cause loss of time and delays in work is not the answer. If there is lost time at work, especially when working at home, the cause for time loss must be identified and alleviated.

Taking care of the things that can stand in the way of having an excellent work record is what follows when finding the lost work time. Just as what was stated in Chapter 4, finding the lost time is gaining time for the future.

Author's Anecdote

One time, there was a research project being conducted with a strict timeline in my office. All the preliminary research such as a literature review had to be done before the research project team could formulate research questions, determine the correct theories on which they could base their hypotheses, and create a methodology that made sense for collecting and analyzing data. All systems went smoothly for the first two weeks and then all of a sudden, the project took a turn.

One of my fellow researchers got sick with COVID-19 and did not tell anyone on the team. We grew concerned when this colleague did not show up for the weekly check-in meetings. The fact that our colleague was ill was very concerning and the fact that our project was halted was also a concern. In this case, we did not know why we were not making progress until someone on the team got a text message from our ill colleague. It took ten days before anyone knew what was happening. The ten days were lost time. When we finally discovered why the project was not moving forward, we could see that we needed to make adjustments to the assigned roles and responsibilities to make it possible to complete the project on time.

In this case, the lost time was found, the reason for it was handled, and the project made progress. Our colleague rejoined us when he was feeling better and the completed project was delivered on time to the leadership depending on it. Also, this was a lesson to institute a policy for the future whereby notice of illness or any other factor disrupting the progress of a project is communicated immediately to the team project leader.

There is a trust factor in working remotely and the way time is spent is paramount to the continuance of that trust. An online employer must have trust and confidence in their remote employee for the working relationship to flourish. Not losing time in the first place is the goal that can be accomplished and needs to be accomplished. But if time gets lost, backtrack to the point where it was lost, learn what happened, and reverse that occurrence from happening. It may seem too simple, but it is necessary to preserve and protect work time, and the trust between the remote worker and online employer.

7.3 How to Regain Trust With Time

If trust is broken, so is the working relationship. The best thing to do in this case is to let time take its course. What this means is you can rebuild trust over time with intentional actions and a contrite attitude. If there was a moment in time when you were distracted to the point of losing concentration and focus and made a terrible error by which your work reputation suffered, there is a way to regain your reputation and the trust of your employer.

This is especially the case for using the time-blocking and P.A.U.S.E methods to work more excellently and accurately. This is the way you can earn back the trust and confidence that was lost with the blunder, and not blunder again in the future.

Just like a person forgetting an item for an event, such as forgetting the tent for a camping trip, will never do that again, a remote worker that blundered at their job can ensure there will be no more blunders.Bu using the techniques of both time-blocking and P.A.U.S.E., you can be assured that your work is reviewed, re-written (if needed), and is of high quality when submitted.

Consider this Scenario:

Jennifer has a reputation at work for being the best conflict negotiator for the firm. She is trusted to resolve customer complaints in a timely manner to the great satisfaction of the customer. Many customers remarked how well she handled their complaints to her boss, Jose. Since Jennifer is so good at her job, Jose gives her the most difficult customers to resolve their issues. Jennifer loves her job and feels very fulfilled every time she resolves a customer's complaint successfully. She especially appreciates being trusted to handle the most difficult cases and is recently awarded a pay raise and promotion. All is going well, until the day when she loses focus and concentration and causes a huge blunder for the firm.

Jennifer was handed a case in which the customer complained about the ill-treatment by a sales representative. This type of case needs sensitivity and confidentiality and usually, that is exactly how Jennifer handles a case such as this. But, when something happened in Jennifer's personal life that caused her to lose concentration and focus, she mishandled the case, causing the customer to be more upset and accidentally ruined a colleague's reputation in the process. Now, the company not only had to deal with an upset customer, but a really upset employee, and boss too.

Jennifer sent a resolution report to the wrong email distribution because she learned that her sister's son committed suicide. She was the favorite aunt to her sister's son and was utterly devastated to learn what happened. She could not think straight and in that state of mind, continued through the process she did hundreds of times, only this time, it was done incorrectly.

Jennifer was so utterly ashamed and embarrassed that she came really close to resigning from her position. She was so upset about making the customer, colleague, and boss upset, that she became very depressed and lost confidence in herself. So, this error was not just affecting the firm, it was affecting her too. It was also affecting time. The customer's time with the firm is cut short because they are no longer a customer of the firm since the matter was not resolved and was instead, escalated. The colleague's time is lost due to the fallout of the lost reputation caused by Jennifer's actions. And let's consider the lost time of Jose's productivity for all the time spent reporting the incident and answering for what happened to his superiors. Since this customer was one of the most influential customers of the firm, the firm may even lose more customers.

This blunder cost time and money and could have been avoided. Using the time-blocking method, Jennifer would have kept track of the filing date of the customer's complaint and the actions that needed to be taken confidentially. Using the P.A.U.S.E. method, Jennifer would have noticed the error she was making before she made it.

Does this scenario sound familiar? Maybe it was an email sent to the wrong address or address distribution; maybe it was an unfulfilled promise or late delivery of a needed deliverable. Or maybe it was a mistake in how an incident was handled with the client and the matter was broadcasted on social media, creating a media circus. Whatever the blunder, there was likely a fallout and lost time.

So, since this chapter is all about how to regain lost time [and trust], let's again look into the case of Jennifer's blunder. Doing this allows us to pinpoint the moment in time when tthe ime was lost to gain time in the future.

Jennifer needed to block out time for writing, reviewing, and sending the report. There are three phases to resolving the case. The report starts with the customer's complaint and the interview that follows during the investigation about what happened to cause the customer's dissatisfaction. Next, the investigation is reported to all the parties involved. Then, the resolution concession is made to the customer, accepted by the customer, and added to the report. Before sending in the report, it is reviewed, and all the parties' email addresses are listed on the front sheet. Using the time-blocking method, all of these phases are time-blocked and carried out in order and at the right time for handling the case. The P.A.U.S.E. method allows for a split instant to make sure that all the T's are crossed and the I's dotted leaving no chance for error.

Time blocking allows keeping track of where Jennifer is in the process of the case, and P.A.U.S.E. assures that the report is written correctly, especially the list of parties and their email addresses. In Jennifer's devasted state of mind, sent in the report before all the phases had been completed. Jennifer could have avoided this blunder by using the time blocking and P.A.U.S.E. methods. So, you can now see, how using these methods not only prevents blunders that cause loss of time, but also protects work reputations, and prevents the loss of customers.

Knowing at what point in time things went wrong gives us time in the future. Jennifer has time to regain her reputation, trust, and confidence as she continues to do her work with excellence using the time-blocking and P.A.U.S.E. methods. If you can relate to this scenario you can consider using these methods in your work life. By using both the time-blocking method and combining it with the P.A.U.S.E. method, you will never be in a position of embarrassment or unfulfilled deliverables when working for your online employer.

Discussion Questions

1. What do you need to do to make your work-at-home experience satisfactory to you and your employer?

2. What can you do to preserve and protect the trust of your employer to spend their time wisely and productively?

3. Are you aware of the positive and negative synchronicity taking place as you work at home?

4. What does finding lost time mean to you and your life?

Quiz

1. Negative synchronicity with the work schedule is disconcerting and must be handled multiple events at a time.

    a. True

    b. False

2. An online employer must have _____ and _____ in their remote employee for the working relationship to flourish.

    a. trust, confidence

    b. respect, positivity

    c. confidence, respect

3. Observing synchronicity with the work schedule means _____ seeing the meaningful events taking place within the work session.

    a. intentionally

    b. deterministically

    c. dramatically

4. Take _____ that does away with time wasters.

    a. time

    b. action

    c. plans

5. If the time gets lost, then more than likely an _____ job task is the result.

   a. unscheduled

   b. unfulfilled

   c. unassigned

6. Time _____ need to be identified and swiftly handled.

   a. eaters

   b. wasters

   c. blockers

7. Wasting time is the same as losing time.

   a. True

   b. False

8. If time gets lost, _____ to the time when it was lost.

   a. backtrack

   b. complain

   c. neither answer is correct

9. Dealing with the _____ of distractions and things that waste a remote worker's time is paramount to their ongoing success with their online employer.

   a. causes

   b. ways

   c. methods

10. Intentionally seeing the meaningful events taking place within the work session is _____.

    a. syncopation

    b. synchronicity

    c. synching

Answers	1 – b	2 – a	3 – a	4 – b	5 – b
	6 – b	7 – a	8 – c	9 – a	10 – b

Chapter Summary

◆ Act immediately when you realize that time is lost.

◆ Make a list and be observant of the events taking place in the day deliberately and with determination to ensure that time spent at work and home is synchronous to the satisfaction of the remote employee and online employer.

◆ Dealing with the causes of distractions and things that waste a remote worker's time is paramount to their ongoing success with their online employer.

◆ There is a trust factor in working remotely and the way time is spent is paramount to the continuance of that trust.

Part 3: Time Management for the Employee-Entrepreneur

This part of the book will help an employee-entrepreneur who owns a business while still working at a job to manage their time. It goes through the steps it takes to make the time count as a family person, worker, and budding entrepreneur. By following these steps, you will be organized and will be able to juggle all the balls successfully.

The key learning objectives include:

- How to make a plan for the week to include prioritizing tasks needed to fulfill home, work, and business obligations

- How to maintain the discipline to follow through with the plan

- How to ensure all obligations are being met

- How to ensure the dream of owning your business comes true

Making an income working for someone is a means of support, but having an additional income from running a sole proprietorship, or working as a business partner helps make ends meet more easily. Owning a business needs planning and saving. Planning for what product or service will be produced or delivered, how the operation will be run, who the key players will be, who the customers will be, and how much start-up capital it will take. All this planning takes time. To that end, time spent from the moment being awake to the moment of being asleep matters greatly. To have a business and be an employee simultaneously takes skilled time management.

Chapter **8**

Tips for Mastering Time in the Day (Starting With a Plan for the Week)

So, you have decided to start a business. You are about to embark on a journey that is challenging and rewarding. Now, in addition to working as an employee, you need to have the time it takes to start and operate your own business. Building off what was covered in Part 1 and Part 2 of this book, we continue the discussion of how to block, monitor, and manage time in the workday to our employer's advantage and to our entrepreneurial advantage. By using these techniques, you will be amazed at how effortless it is to have the time to take the steps needed to start a new business.

Key learning objectives should include the reader's understanding of the following:

- How mastering time with prioritization makes it possible to work and plan a business

- How with determination, it is possible to divide the day and fulfill all needs, wants, and obligations

- How to manage and monitor where the time is spent as a budding entrepreneur

- How to remain in control of the time each day and use it to your advantage

- How to preserve and protect your work image, your dream of owning a business, and the quality of your work and family relationships

When planning to own a business, there is a lot of preliminary work to be done before filling out the forms to formalize the business. You need to research to be sure that what you plan to market meets a need. This is called market research and it takes place through online research, talking to people, and observation. That takes time. So how is it possible to squeeze in this research while working full-time and meeting work and family obligations?

You use time blocking and create a matrix with three columns: Home, Work, and Business. If you were attending school or college or any other type of training when there are class assignments, studying, and group work involved, you can add a column for school/college too.

To know what to put in this time-blocking matrix, you need to know the steps it takes to start a business and the actions associated with those steps. You may consider reading the book: *Business Plan Essentials You Always Wanted to Know* and see what the steps are for starting and sustaining your business. But, for the purpose of helping you manage your time so that you can take these steps, consider learning a little bit about these steps from the examples provided in this chapter.

In the same way that you learned how to work backward, manage, and monitor time in Part 1 and Part 2 of the book, we use the same techniques when blocking time and managing it for the purpose of working, fulfilling home obligations, and starting your own business.

Use intentionality when making a list of three columns for each obligation within one week. There is a column for home obligations, work obligations, and business obligations. In each of the columns are tasks associated with each of the different obligations. See the chart as an example.

Table 8.1   Planning a week to accomplish priorities

To-do items for the week of July 24-July 31	Home	Work	Business
Activity	**Paint the fence**	**Complete the software coding for the new app (due July 28)**	**Do market research**
Time to do the activity	*After dinner Tuesday, July 26*	*Working 9 am - 2 pm Monday, July 25 and completing project Wednesday, July 27)*	*After 2 pm Monday, Tuesday, and Wednesday*
Activity	**Mend the porch screen**	**Review co-worker's software project (on July 28)**	**Get EIN**
Time to do the activity	*Sunday, July 24*	*After completing my project - will review co-worker's project*	*While taking a lunch break Monday, July 25*
Activity	**Date night**		**Complete and file Articles of Incorporation (self-imposed deadline July 30)**
Time to do the activity	*Friday night, July 29*		*July 29 during lunch break*

[The bold print is the task associated with the category and the italics underneath is the time allotted to complete the task.]

Consider this scenario: A business analyst, married with two children in pre-kindergarten and working for a corporation wants to earn an additional income as a business consultant in their own sole proprietorship. After researching what an operating budget would be and the amount of start-up capital needed, the business analyst makes a three-column list for each day of the week. In the work obligation column are the daily deliverables, and in the home obligation list are the home chores and tasks for assisting with running the household. The third column is filled with tasks including market research, writing the business plan, building a website, and Facebook page, lining up all the needed social media accounts, creating a company LinkedIn page, and making sure to deposit money in the savings account that will be used to cover the start-up costs for the consulting business.

Now that the list is made, it is time to act upon it by allocating the appropriate time it takes to fulfill all three columns of obligations as the business analyst goes about the day with determination and discipline.

Consider what would happen if the list were not made. The obligations may or may not get met, and the money it takes may or may not be saved. The intention of having the business consulting business becomes a pipedream, remaining unfulfilled. So, let us turn our attention now to the next step in the process of fulfilling the intention of owning a business and prioritizing tasks and time.

8.1 Manage Priorities (Work Obligations-Capital Building-Play to Relax)

Prioritizing tasks first takes place with the decision as to which task is the most important and which task is the least important. This is sometimes easier said than done. The Indeed Editorial Team published an extremely helpful list of 11 items to consider when prioritizing tasks.[13]

1. Use a priority matrix: create rows and columns and name the task and the category it fits into (i.e., home, work, business) and rate them according to the level of urgency and importance.

2. Number your priorities: a rating of priority, from 1 (the most important).

3. Make a prioritized task list each day, based on the time it takes to complete them.

4. Prioritize the most important tasks (self-explanatory).

5. Pick a single focus: a task that is very important and must be done in a timely manner.

6. Create a master list and break it down: monthly goals, weekly goals, and daily goals.

7. Use the Ivy Lee method: suggest writing your top six most important tasks at the end of each day. Number the tasks 1 to

---

13. Indeed Editorial Team (23 November 2021) 11 Prioritization Strategies to Help You Arrange Your Tasks. Retrieved from www.indeed.com

6 with 1 being the most important. Once done, move on to the next in the list until all six are completed.

8. Use the ABCDE [Brian Tracy's] method: "A" tasks have the highest priority to be done first.

9. For larger goals, use [Warren Buffet's] two-list strategy (prioritizing long-term goals)

   Warren Buffet's two-list strategy:

   Step 1: Write down your top 25 career goals on a single piece of paper.

   Step 2: Circle only your top five options.

   Step 3: Put the top five on one list and the remaining 20 on a second list. Only touch the other 20 once the top five goals are fully accomplished.

10. Change priorities if necessary (self-explanatory).

11. Prioritize your important work during your most productive hours: based on the time of day (or night) when you are the most alert and motivated.

The list of tasks for a budding entrepreneur may include depositing money into the bank account and keeping some time for self-care. The time taken to build a business is stressful and you need an outlet to release the stress. This can be a time for you to spend at your leisure (like a date night). It must be intentionally scheduled and intentionally planned so this must be in one of the three columns.

The manner in which you decide what item gets the most priority depends on your situation. Are you preparing to own a business that someone may sell to you and there is a deadline connected with the deal? Are you self-imposing a date for opening a business? Or - is there a particular date that is special to you to open your business? Whatever the case, you need to include the time for planning and strategizing in your weekly time-blocking chart. As was shared in Part 1 of this book, working backward gives you a plan and strategy by which you can take preliminary steps in time to open your business.

Example:

You are a military veteran transitioning from active duty to working full-time as an insurance sales representative. You also have a dream to have your own computer repair business since you are a master at fixing and troubleshooting computer hardware and software issues. You helped many other fellow military members while serving in the military and you dreamed of doing this as a business after leaving the military. But, of course, you needed employment to pay the bills and build up the capital it takes to start a business.

Now, you are reading this book curious to see how working backward and using the time-blocking method is going to help you fulfill your entrepreneurial goal.

You want to open your computer-repair business on the next Veteran's Day i.e. November 11. This is what the Gantt Chart will look like for you to open your computer repair business.

Table 8.2   **Gantt Chart for opening a computer repair business**

Tasks for opening a business on Nov 11					
(Planning and preparing starts on April 15)	April 15 – 30	May – July	August – September	October	November
Do market research	▓				
Save money to cover the cost of startup	▓	▓			
Research what forms and licenses are needed to formalize and legalize the business meeting federal and state requirements		▓			
Obtain the forms			▓		
Obtain an Employee Identification Number (EIN) from the IRS.Gov website			▓		
Complete the forms and pay the filing fees			▓		
Write a business plan. Get a website and a social media and start a marketing campaign					▓

Seeing the preliminary steps it takes before being ready to service customers gives you an idea of the work involved in making the business dream a reality. Now let's see how to further time-block the week of October 10 – 17.

8.2 Dividing the Day

Divide the day and follow through with the three different columns that were created in table 8.2 according to the priority set in each category and block time accordingly. To clarify, table 8.2 is the task list and the order in which the tasks need to be done before starting the business. That is a priority listing of tasks. You decide which time of the day a task gets completed.

Consider this scenario: You are married with children ages 5 and 7. You changed jobs and are now working for a corporation as a software engineer. But, it is your dream to own a business of fixing or troubleshooting computer hardware or software issues. To prepare for the opening of this business in the month of October, forms need to be filled out, and the filing fees need to be paid. Being prudent, you make a three-column list with the intention to be productive by covering all the bases for home, work, and future business.

By following the method of prioritizing your tasks, you carve out a schedule with the prioritization list to ensure that the tasks in each of the columns get done in the order needed. Dividing the tasks into the days they are going to be accomplished, with you deciding what part of the day to do them, all tasks for accomplishing the goals are managed with ease. See how the below chart is developed.

Table 8.3   **Time-blocking chart to accomplish priorities within a week**

Dates	Home	Work	Business
Sunday, **October 10**	Mend the porch screen		
Monday, **October 11**		Work on a software project and complete it by Wednesday, Oct 12	Complete the form for EIN
Tuesday, **October 12**	Paint the fence after dinner		
Wednesday, **October 13**		Review tasks Mon-Wed and do what is not yet done	Complete the state registration forms and pay the filing fees
Thursday, **October 14**		Review co-worker's project	
Friday, **October 15**	Date night!		
Saturday, **October 16**			Make sure the Articles of Incorporation are filed with the state
Sunday, **October 17**	Relax!		

[See that each of the prioritized taskings takes place on a day within the week it is due. See too that in doing this intentional organization, there is plenty of flexibility for doing other things. In other words, this method is not so regimental that you may feel militarized and not have the freedom to spend time playing video games, socializing, etc. This method has plenty of room to spend time as you want to while accomplishing what you intend to accomplish].

It takes intentionality and discipline to create this chart and perseverance to implement it. Now, we can take this a step further and time-block a particular day. As a software engineer, you are working at home developing software as a team member for most projects, and as a team leader for two projects.

Table 8.4 shows what the time blocking would look like for this scenario:

| Table 8.4 | Time-blocking chart for completing work, home, and business tasks in a day |

Time of day: October 13	Work task	Home task	Business start-up task
8:00 am – 8:30 am	Login to company portal and read email messages		
8:30 am – 9:30 am	Attend team meeting		
9:30 am – 10:00 am	Review task guidelines and begin working on software project		
10:00 am – 10:30 am	Meet with a member of team project		
10:30 am – 11:00 am			Go to the IRS. Gov website and complete the application online and obtain the EIN
11:00 am – 12:00 noon	Continue working on software project		
12:00 pm – 12:30 pm	Travel to school		
12:30 pm – 1:00 pm		Eat lunch with child at school	
1:00 pm – 1:30 pm	Travel home from school		
1:30 pm – 2:30 pm	Lead project team meeting		
2:30 pm – 3:30 pm	Continue working on Software projects		
3:30 pm – 4:00 pm		Chop lettuce for taco night	
4:00 pm – 4:30 pm			Go to the state registration website and complete the forms and pay the filing fee

With time blocking, all needs are met and obligations are fulfilled. It is possible to juggle all the balls of home, work, and business without them letting them fall to the ground unfulfilled. It takes effort and willpower along with intentionality and discipline to create the chart and follow it.

You decide the priority of what needs to be done and by what date. You then decide how to divide the time working backward, fitting in the time it takes to complete work tasks, meet home obligations, and stay true to your dream of owning a business. It is not enough to make a chart; you have to efficiently organize it too. With the organization of thought and deed, it is possible to have employment, a family, and keep your dream alive of owning a business.

Discussion Questions

1. Can you picture yourself finding the time needed to start a business? What does that look like for you?

2. Was there a time when you wanted to start a business and said to yourself, "I can't find the time to start a business?" If yes, do you think it is possible to now start your business with the methods and techniques mentioned in the book?

Quiz

1. _____ is the best method to use to squeeze in the time prepare to open a business.

   a. Monitoring

   b. Managing

   c. Time-blocking

2. Managing and monitoring time and making sure that all obligations are met is an impossible thing to do.

   a. True

   b. False

3. It takes intentionality and discipline to create a time-blocking chart and _____ to implement it.

   a. grit

   b. perseverance

   c. willpower

4. Following the method of prioritizing your tasks, you carve out a schedule with the _____ list to ensure that the tasks in each of the columns get done in the order needed.

   a. prioritization

   b. perseverance

   c. performance

5. The manner in which you decide what item gets the most priority does not depend on your situation.

   a. True

   b. False

6. Use _____ when making a list of three columns for each obligation within one week.

   a. perseverance

   b. intentionality

   c. grit

7. _____ gives you a plan and strategy by which the preliminary steps are taken in time to open your business.

   a. Time blocking

   b. Working backward

   c. Managing time

8. When planning to own a business, there is a lot of _____ work to be done before filling out the forms to formalize the business.

   a. preliminary

   b. busy

   c. spendy

9. You need to _____ to be sure that what you plan to market meets a need.

    a. research

    b. willpower

    c. way power

10. To know what to put in a time block, you should know the steps it takes to start a business and the actions associated with those steps.

    a. True

    b. False

Answers	1 – c	2 – b	3 – b	4 – a	5 – b
	6 – b	7 – b	8 – a	9 – a	10 – a

Chapter Summary

◆ Managing priorities is a way to master time in the day.

◆ Dividing the week's tasks for work, home, and business is a way to organize priorities for each category of obligation.

◆ With blocking time for the week and the day, it is possible to complete those tasks that fulfill and meet expectations of work, home, and your business.

This page is intentionally left blank

Chapter 9

Tricks to Use for Being in Control of Time

As a budding entrepreneur with employment and home obligations, the need for making sure time does not get away from you is paramount to succeeding in your goal to have your own business. For this to happen, intentionality, determination, diligence, and perseverance should take center stage in your life. Working every day of every moment with the intention to be disciplined to follow the timeline you set is the first step in this trick. The next step that follows is having the determination to follow the prioritized plan without hesitation or distraction. This is where diligence comes into the picture. Being diligent means being watchful for things that come up and might distract you. Being this observant with diligence allows you to go into discipline drive and manage these distractions quickly so they do not take away your precious time. Finally, perseverance is necessary when implementing this trick for staying in control of time. It is not easy to get yourself in the habit of being intentional as to how you spend your day. But it is possible to do this. Many phenomenally successful people do.

Key learning objectives should include the reader's understanding of the following:

- How intentionality, determination, diligence, and perseverance work together to make a dream of owning a business a reality

- How to manage and monitor the events in a day to stay on track with meeting goals and obligations

- How to manage and monitor where the time is spent as an employee and entrepreneur

- How to remain in control of friendships and family relationships while juggling obligations

- How to preserve and protect your work image and the quality of your work

9.1 Manage and Monitor the Moments

It takes a lot of patience, practice, and positivity to manage and monitor the moments in the day if you are working a job and for your own business. It is a balancing act. Managing and monitoring the moments in the day gets easier when you are organized, such as using the table 8.1 chart for outlining the week and the table 8.2 chart for organizing what takes place on the day of the week. Of course, there must be a willingness and a mindset to do so.

Without blocking your time, there are many moments in the day that seem to disappear without a trace. Juggling work and home obligations is not an easy thing to do, especially when you are also adding the startup of a business to the mix.

Imagine actually juggling three balls labeled home, work, and business. Now imagine throwing them up in the air and one of them drops to the ground. When that happens, there are unfulfilled and unmet obligations that no doubt will lead to hurt feelings and disappointment. If one of those balls was "work" then your boss must deal with an unmet deliverable(s), and you know what that could be to the future of your employment. So, knowing how to manage and monitor the moments in the day, with intentional and disciplined time blocking is essential to ensure that all three balls: work, home, and business are juggled without dropping any of them.

The best way to manage and monitor the time in the day is to plan and prepare for them in advance. Think short-term and long-term at the same time when making a list of priorities, and then block your time according to the list.

The list of priorities for home usually follows suit with the expectations of your family members and friends. Things, like mowing the lawn, driving your child to practice, shopping on the weekend, date nights, cleaning the garage, pulling weeds in the garden, going fishing, camping, boating, attending children's sports and concerts, etc., are all particularly important to family relationships and must be listed among the other tasks for work and business.

Work priorities are of course in accordance with the deliverables requested by the employer. If you work autonomously and set your own work hours, then there is an even greater responsibility to maintain the trust and confidence of your employer. With that being said, priorities for your work must be listed and adhered to in the time-blocking chart. Only with time blocking is it possible to ensure the deliverables are completed and submitted on time to satisfy your manager.

Then we come to the third column of priorities which includes the steps it takes to start and operate a business. They are outlined in the matrix of 8.2. Keep in mind the tasks associated with the paperwork to formalize a new business with the federal and state government. There are many more tasks such as opening a bank account, writing a business plan that includes a financial, operational, and marketing plan, and selecting and retaining an accountant, lawyer, and perhaps a partner to work with you. That all takes time and if it were not part of a priority list, it might not even get accomplished.

So, with all three columns of priorities completed, it is time to take this list into a time-blocking chart. Not only using time blocking, but also time mentality.

Time mentality is the experience of knowing how time is spent. Unlike time perception and time consciousness, time mentality is what occurs when someone monitors their use of time and is in control of it. This is the term used when describing the intentional actions that occur within an allotted time frame.

9.2 It is a Marathon, Not a Sprint (Mind Control)

Thinking you are going to start a business in the same month you were thinking about it is unrealistic, yet some people get impatient when it does not happen that quickly. They get so impatient that their mood turns sour, and they become stressed. Therefore, this portion of the chapter discusses the mindset an employee who is a budding entrepreneur.

Getting anything accomplished takes the gumption and willpower to see through it. Phillip C. McGraw ("Dr. Phil") said, "Life's a marathon, not a sprint." This was phrased in his book, "Self Matters: Creating your life from the inside out."[14] Dr. Phil pointed out that we as human beings need to be aware that we are not victims of circumstance, instead, we are designers and producers of our own lives. As designers of our own lives and destiny, we get to say what we want and do what it takes to get what we want. Taking this into consideration, as budding business owners, we follow through with our plan with action steps. Those action steps are taken amidst ensuring that our home and work obligations are met. So, having the mindset in place, that achieving the goal of owning a business will eventually happen, we live into the dream by planning, acting, and following through every step of the way.

It takes time and effort to see these goals and dreams come to fruition. You will need to juggle work, home, and business simultaneously without dropping any ball. Because dropping any ball means someone or something is at risk of not getting what it needs or wants. With all this going on in your thought life, it is no wonder why so many goals and dreams do not see the light of day.

Having the time mentality with all these thoughts is what allows you to juggle the balls, take a breath, and relax in the process. Having the priorities listed and time blocked is what

---

14. McGraw, Phillip C. (13, November 2001) Life Matters: Creating your life from the inside out. Simon & Schuster Publisher

allows you to follow through with the juggling with confidence and no stress. You can easily see in the time blocks for the day, week, and perhaps even for the month how all the tasks for home, work, and business get done. You see now why it is possible to work as an employee and operate as an entrepreneur with no stress? It is also possible to be an employee, a family member, and budding entrepreneur without losing friends or family relationships. That is possible when the time spent with friends and family is included in the time blocks. I developed day, week, and monthly time blocking charts since the moment I learned this technique. That is why it is possible for me to , teach a full load of college classes, work full-time as a data analyst, be a loving and devoted spouse, mother, grandmother, and great-grandmother, a businessperson, and leader of a non-profit organization. Juggling all these balls at the same time without any of them dropping takes mastering the moments in the day, every day!

Author's Anecdote

There was a time when I attempted to juggle work, home, school, and a business but failed. Yes - before learning the time-blocking method, I was taking classes to get my MBA. At that time, I was working full-time, taking a full load of graduate classes online, was a spouse, mother, and grandmother, and was a leader of a nonprofit organization too. It was actually during the time when class assignments were falling by the wayside, reports for work were not getting done on time, and promises made to my spouse, children, and grandchildren were remaining unfulfilled, that the technique of blocking time was shown to me.

At first, I looked at this technique as something that takes up too much time and would require too much discipline. But, when the group assignment was not ready on time, and my employer placed me on an improvement plan, is when I took another look at this time-blocking method and started making my priority list.

I made the list, checked it against my work, school, and home calendars, and then proceeded to make a time-blocking chart first for the week, and then drilled it down to each day of the week. When there was a long-range plan to accomplish a project at work, I used the time-blocking method and working backward method to ensure that all my obligatory tasks for that project are done ahead of schedule (I had to make up for lost time for not having in my reports on time). It became easier to keep track of what needed to be done and what had been done.

So, at first, I was not enthused about sitting down and making a priority list. But, after a couple of incidents that were embarrassing and could have been avoided, I mustered intentionality and discipline and made my list of priorities, and fit them into a time block. What happened next made me regret not using this method before.

Using the time-blocking method and working backward method, it was possible to juggle all the balls and not have any of them drop to the ground. In the beginning, I was attempting to take care of all my obligations and meet all the expectations associated with the obligations for home, work, business, and school. I was failing miserably until I started blocking time according to my priorities. Then suddenly, there were no unsatisfied employers, family, and school classmates, and my life was less stressful.

Discussion Questions

1. What business are you planning to own and operate?

2. When do you foresee the opening of your business?

3. How are you planning to juggle the balls of home, work, and business without them dropping to the ground?

Quiz

━━

1. It takes _____ and _____ to make your list of priorities and then place them in time blocks.

   a. intention, grit

   b. intention, discipline

   c. intention, determination

2. Getting anything accomplished takes the gumption and willpower to see it through.

   a. True

   b. False

3. It takes a lot of patience, practice, and _____ to manage and monitor the moments in the day if you are working at a job and for your own business.

   a. perseverance

   b. positivity

   c. poise

4. Monitoring the moments in a day is a _____ act.

   a. balancing

   b. backward

   c. brilliant

5. Managing and monitoring the moments in the day gets
   _____ when you are organized.

   a. harder

   b. faster

   c. easier

6. _____ priorities are in accordance with the deliverables
   requested by the employer.

   a. Work

   b. Home

   c. Business

7. _____ priorities are in keeping with family and friend's
   expectations and your obligations to them.

   a. Social

   b. Home

   c. Work

8. When juggled balls drop to the ground, there are unfulfilled
   and unmet obligations that no doubt will lead to hurt
   feelings and disappointment.

   a. True

   b. False

9. Juggling work and home obligations is not an easy thing to do, especially when you are also adding the _____ of a business to the mix.

   a. startup

   b. operation

   c. plan

10. Having _____, is what allows you to consistently monitor how time is used, and successfully juggle the balls in life.

    a. good intention

    b. pipe dreaming

    c. time mentality

Answers	1 – b	2 – a	3 – b	4 – a	5 – c
	6 – a	7 – b	8 – a	9 – a	10 – c

Chapter Summary

◆ Being in control of every moment of every day takes intentionality and discipline.

◆ After making a list of three columns of priorities for home, work, and business, it is time for time blocking.

◆ Time blocking takes the list of priorities and places them in a block of time to be accomplished.

◆ Blocking time for your priorities is what makes it possible to juggle all the balls in life without any of them dropping to the ground.

This page is intentionally left blank

Chapter **10**

Techniques for Finding the Time When Time is Lost

OK, we all know that best intentions are sometimes just that - "best intentions." So, we give ourselves a break when something falls through the cracks, such as lost time. We see that time was lost to help us learn lessons and make sure not to waste or lose time again. Lessons learned are a wonderful time recovery mechanism. We know what *not to do* and what we *should* do next time!

The best way to find the time that was lost is to consult the priorities and task chart. There you can plainly see whether the tasks are being done or not. You have the power to make sure the task is getting done as planned and prioritized.

Key learning objectives should include the reader's understanding of the following:

- How momentary check-in with priorities helps find the time that was lost

- How finding lost time gains time for the future

- How to maintain the commitment to yourself without losing time

- How to live your dream of owning and operating a business without stress

- How to preserve and protect your work image and the quality of your work

10.1 Momentary Check-in With Priorities

Working with the three-column checklist, it is possible to see where time may have been lost and recover from that moment. Therefore, on Wednesday in the chart of Fig. 8.2, there is a place in the time of the week to take inventory of the tasks in the columns, and any task still not done, gets done on Wednesday. Any task not yet accomplished, such as painting the fence, gets tended to with the intention of completing the task. This check-in with the tasks in accordance with the priorities in each category of obligation gets accomplished and is not missed. Imagine what could happen if the priorities and the associated tasks were not organized. Oh, yes, you know what would happen.

Losing time is a terrible waste of time, unless, finding it makes it possible to gain it for the future. The only way to know where the time was lost, and how to find it, is to look at the time-blocking chart. What was it that was not done? When was supposed to be done? We are human beings and not capable of consistently monitoring the time and where it goes, no matter how determined they are, no matter how determined we are. We get easily distracted, dissuaded, and lose focus. When that happens, our best intentions are laid aside. When our intentions are laid aside, what we meant to have happened, does not happen. Then, by having things that were meant to be done and are not done, we are faced with the reality that we lost time. Where was the time lost? We need to know this and not ignore it so that we can gain it back for the future.

Wednesday is in the middle of the week so for the lost time of things not done, it is possible to schedule them to be done in the remaining days of the week. So, if there was a report that needed to be drafted the following Monday, and it was not done by Wednesday, you can shift things around and make that report a top priority. As things are being done (or not done), the priority list changes, and so does the time blocking.

Blocking time for your priorities to be accomplished is the best way not to lose time, but also to find the time that was lost. You may recall that it takes intentionality and discipline to create a list of priorities and then to follow through with doing what is on the list of priorities within the assigned block of time; so if there is a task or assignment lost, there is lost time, which must be identified and regained.

As discussed in the previous chapters, the act of finding lost time takes time, but in the end, regains time for the future. This is only possible when the tasks and assignments are assigned in a block of time. When the assignments and tasks are in time blocks and are not done, it is easy to see where the time was lost. Now, what you do with that information makes or breaks the regaining of the time in the future.

When you can see where the time was lost, the next thing to see is how the time was lost. Was it a distraction? Was it an oversight? Why did you miss the task or assignment? Why was the task or assignment not accomplished? Maybe you needed more time for completing the task or assignment. Sometimes, we get weary and discouraged if what needs to be done is not all done in a certain amount of time as expected. When this happens, we lose focus and start to doubt our ability to complete the task or assignment. This is only a natural reaction to seeing that the time allotted for accomplishing a task or assignment was not reasonable and there needs to be more time and effort to get it done.

Whatever the cause for a task or assignment to remain undone, the fact that there is an unfulfilled task or assignment means there is a loss of time. This cannot be ignored. This loss of time needs to be addressed, identified, and dealt with. Maybe more time needs to be allotted. Perhaps the cause of the distraction needs to be identified and addressed. Whatever the case, the situation of an unfulfilled task or assignment is one that indicates time was lost. As such, and in the interest of staying true to your intentions, the lost time needs to be investigated and identified so that measures are taken to prevent more lost time in the future. Preventing losing time makes it possible to find the time for the future and stay true to what you are committed to doing.

10.2 Make a Commitment to Yourself

Dr. Phil encourages us to be responsible for how our lives turn out. He literally prompts us to be committed to ourselves and to our futures. This is making a commitment to ourselves to see to it that what we want to happen in our life does happen. Even if life throws us a curveball and our world gets topsy-turvy, we still can have control over our lives, just like we have control over the time in our lives.

The distraction that occurs when life gets topsy-turvy or does not go as expected is something that can throw all intentions off-track. If you intended to open your business in 6 months, and 6 months later you are still struggling with raising the capital to cover the startup costs, you would allow not fulfilling the expectation to become a distraction. Not fulfilling a self-imposed timeline is often reacted to with disappointment and discouragement. This is what we do when things do not happen in the timeframe we expect. However, instead of treating the unfulfilled timeframe as a disappointment and discouragement, why not treat it as a determination and diligence factor for mustering intentionality with discipline and setting another timeline, working backward, and accomplishing the goal? Just because the first timeframe did not produce what was expected does not mean the goal is any less valid.

Your goal of owning and operating your business is valid and deserves all the attention and time it takes to make it real. Having a business where you are in charge, you are the boss, and another income provider is attainable, with time. It takes time to plan, execute the plan, make preparations, and then eventually operate the business. The commitment it takes drives the intentionality which drives the determination which drives the discipline to do what it takes, and the time it takes to be ready to own and operate your business (or organization). The discussion has been what to do with the time you have in a day, week, or month to own and operate your business, but this also applies to owning and operating a not-for-profit business or an organization by which you plan to make a difference in people's lives, sustain the environment, or for whatever reason your organization or not-for-profit business exists. Whether the business is for-profit or not-for-profit, the time and the steps it takes to go from an idea to a realized dream are the same. The level of commitment you must be seeing in your dream becomes a reality too.

10.3 Your Time to Shine

What do you plan to do with "your dash?" You know, it is the "dash" that appears on a tombstone indicating the time a person was on this planet from the moment they are born into this life, to the moment they pass on and leave this life. So, what does that look like for you? As you read this, are you satisfied with the way your dash is going? Do you have any unfulfilled dreams? Are you shaking your head as you look at the calendar filled with all the obligations you currently have, thinking, "I don't have the time it takes to make my dreams a reality?" If this describes you and your dash, you are not alone. According to an article in CBS, "In 2021, a share of 81 percent in the population aged 18 to 24 said they were unhappy; 86 percent adults reported that they were unhappy and 84 percent unfulfilled."[15]

Unfulfilled dreams and goals are common. "It is easy to say you'll do something. Another thing is to actually do it." "If you feel like you're meant for something bigger, but you are not moving forward at all, then it is time to look at your day and your time management. You might not even realize that you are wasting time."[16] "Fulfillment starts with finding that balance

15. CBS (2022, April 25) Fewer Young Adults Say They Are Happy. CBS. www.cbs.nl
16. Jenson, M. (2022, June 7) Have an Unfulfilled Life? 7 Reasons Why You're Not Satisfied. *Lifehack.* www.lifehack.org

between what you can and cannot control. That means taking radical responsibility for your behaviors and your decisions."[17] What these quotes are emphasizing is the fact that you can and should have what it is you desire in your lifetime.

Your dash is your time to shine in this lifetime. You are reading this because you are looking for ways to make the time in your dash count toward fulfilling a goal. This chapter addresses the intention to own and operate a business, but when you stop to think about it, working backward, prioritizing, and using the time-blocking method can be applied to any specific goal in life.

The focus needs to be laser-focused on accomplishing your goals and dreams so that the goals and dreams see the light of day. They become real and, in the process, you become happy and feel fulfilled. Tony Robbins said, "The path to success is to take massive action, and setting goals is the first step in turning the invisible into the visible.[18] As you may or may not know, Mr. Robbins is one of the most successful people walking the planet today and it took time and staying true to his intentions to become successful. That is what it takes to have what you want with your dash. Having a lifetime of living your dreams, feeling fulfilled, with no regrets, and never asking "where did the time go?" is possible and even probable with the time management tricks, tips, and techniques that you have learned from reading this book. Go now and make your life into what you have always wanted it to be.

---

17. Christian, L, (2021, March 8) 11 Reasons You Are Feeling Unfulfilled (and What to Do About It). *Soul Salt.* www.soulsalt.com

18. Robbins, T. (2020) Top 20 Motivational Quotes by Tony Robbins Quotes.

Discussion Questions

---

1. How do we ensure that our dream to own and operate a business can manifest when we are working for someone full-time?

2. How is it even possible to juggle and not drop the ball for planning to own a business when there are family and work obligations taking top priority?

3. How do you, as a budding business owner, set priorities to include meeting the home, work, and future business obligations?

Quiz

1. **Without organizing priorities, owning a business is just a**
   _____.

   a. nightmare

   b. pipedream

   c. none of the above

2. **When prioritizing obligations, it helps to have three columns for _____.**

   a. home, work, business

   b. social, gaming, shopping

   c. none of the above.

3. **The best day of the week to use as a check-in on prioritized tasks is _____.**

   a. Friday

   b. Thursday

   c. Wednesday

4. **There is always a way to accomplish the things you want to do.**

   a. True

   b. False

5. Lessons learned are a great _____ mechanism.

   a. time recovery

   b. declared time

   c. lost time

6. The best way to find the time that was lost is _____.

   a. consulting your parents

   b. consulting your friends

   c. consulting the priorities and task chart

7. Getting anything accomplished takes the _____ and _____ to see it through.

   a. gumption, willpower

   b. get up, go

   c. way power, willpower

8. Perseverance is necessary when implementing the trick for staying in control of time.

   a. True

   b. False

9. To make a plan and follow through, it takes _____.

   a. determination

   b. dreaming

   c. discussing

10. For most people, the time it takes to own a business is filled with _____.

   a. dreaming and wishing

   b. planning and saving

   c. planning and dreaming

Answers	1 – b	2 – a	3 – c	4 – a	5 – a
	6 – c	7 – a	8 – a	9 – a	10 – b

Chapter Summary

◆ It is possible to juggle home, work, and future business obligations simultaneously.

◆ It takes prioritizing tasks associated with meeting home, work, and future business obligations.

◆ It takes determination, discipline, and willpower to make the plan and follow through.

Glossary

Determination – the grit and fortitude to make sure that something happens as planned.

Intentionality – a mental state that drives determination.

Fulfillment – the emotion and feeling of good that is accompanied after accomplishing something desired and needed.

Priorities – the order in which tasks are accomplished in accordance with working backward.

Productivity – an outcome or result tangible, qualitative, or quantitative, observed or felt as intended. This is referring to something that is a result of determination and intentionality.

Synchronicity – when there is a connection to something.

Time management – deliberate use of time with monitoring to make sure the time is spent wisely and never wasted or lost.

Bibliography

Albert Einstein Quotes. Retrieved from www.quotefancy.com

Bilanich, Bud (2008) Spend Your Time on The Things That Are Important for Your Success. *Fast Company*. Retrieved from www.fastcompany.com

Carl Jung > Synchronicity. Retrieved from www.carl-jung.net

CBS (2022, April 25) Fewer Young Adults Say They Are Happy. CBS. www.cbs.nl

Christian, L, (2021, March 8) 11 Reasons You Are Feeling Unfulfilled (and What to Do About It). *Soul Salt*. www.soulsalt.com

Finn, Amy (2022) 140 Time Quotes on Making Every Second Count. *Quote Ambition*. Retrieved from www.quoteambition.com

Indeed Editorial Team (23 November 2021) 11 Prioritization Strategies to Help You Arrange Your Tasks. Retrieved from www.indeed.com

Jenson, M. (2022, June 7) Have an Unfulfilled Life? 7 Reasons Why You're Not Satisfied. *Lifehack*. www.indeed.com

Khan, Mohammed (2016) *Mastering Your Time*. CreateSpace Independent Publishing Platform, 62 pages ISBN-10: 1533070113; ISBN-13: 978-1533070111.

McGraw, Phillip C. (13, November 2001) Life Matters: Creating your life from the inside out. Simon & Schuster Publisher

Nemko, Marty (2014) Six Secrets to Making the Most of Your Time. Psychology Today. Retrieved from www.psychologytoday.com

Robbins, T. (2020) Top 20 Motivational Quotes by Tony Robbins Quotes.

Time Flies: U.S. Adults Now Spend Nearly Half a Day Interacting with Media. (July 2018) *The Nielsen Company*. Retrieved from www.nielsen.com

www.ingramcontent.com/pod-product-compliance
Lightning Source LLC
Chambersburg PA
CBHW070337270326
41926CB00017B/3901